GETTING THE JOB YOU *really* WANT

- Discover your best skills
- Choose the best job (the one you can do well and enjoy)
- Get that job fast
- Get ahead on your new job

GETTING
THE JOB
YOU *really* WANT

J. Michael Farr

JIST Works, Inc.
Indianapolis, Indiana

Project Director
Ruth Lister

Editor
Sara Hall

Cover Design
Robert Pawlak

Calligraphy
Robin Brown
Barbara Stoots
Tom Draper

---

*Getting the Job You **Really** Want*
©1991, JIST Works, Inc.,
originally published 1987.

Instructor's Guide: A separate instructor's guide and other instructional aids are available from the publisher. Please contact us for details.

Order Form: See order form on last page.

Send all inquiries to
JIST Works, Inc.
720 North Park Avenue
Indianapolis, IN 46202-3431
(317) 264-3720
ISBN 0-942784-15-4

Table of Contents

Introduction

This is a book for two types of people:

- Those who know what job they want to do
- And those who do not

In either case, **Getting The Job You Really Want** will help. If you don't already have a job objective, this book shows you the major types of jobs available and how to find out more about them.

If you already know the kind of job you want, you can learn more about it—and why you would be good at it.

For everyone, there are valuable sections on identifying your skills, using powerful job-search and interviewing techniques, surviving and succeeding on a job, and much more.

Most people who really *use* this book will get a good job in less time.

Make this book your personal road map to success.

This is a book to be used, not just read. It is designed for you to write in, underline, jot notes in margins—make it your own.

Do all the activities in each chapter before going on to the next. That seems an obvious enough recommendation, but I know you are likely to want to skip ahead to the "good stuff." It's OK to browse ahead, of course, but you really won't be effective in an interview, for example, unless you are thoroughly prepared. *Taking a shortcut could allow someone else to get the job you should have had. . . .*

I wish you well,

Mike Farr

GREAT
EXPECTATIONS

What the Dickens Do Employers Want?

What does work mean to you? Work can be just a way to earn a living. Something you have to do to eat and have a place to live. Or work can be what you enjoy doing. A way to help you to do something you feel is important.

However you feel about work now, your feelings are likely to change over your lifetime.

It's hard to imagine what you will be doing far in the future. But you can be fairly certain that things will change. For example, the U.S. Department of Labor now predicts the average person will change careers five to seven times. And change jobs more often than that!

The average 35-year-old has changed jobs once every year and a half since entering the work force. (Some people change jobs, and even careers, more often than others.) It is very likely that you will change your job many times in your life.

Survival Skills for the Working World

To do well in a competitive and rapidly changing job market, you need a new set of survival skills.

Survival Skills

- A method to help you choose and plan long-term career goals.

- Knowledge of effective job-seeking skills.

- A good understanding of yourself and the right job for you.

- How to succeed on the job once you have it.

- Knowledge of types of jobs and what they require.

All these topics—and many others—are covered in this book. If you do the exercises carefully, you will be better prepared for the working world than 90% of all job seekers.

An Employer's Expectations

To succeed as a job seeker and worker, you need to understand an employer's point of view. Many people feel that an employer thinks differently from the rest of us. But employers are just like you and me. Once you stop to think about what you'd want *your* employees to do, you can figure out what is expected of you as a worker. And knowing what employers want will help you to present yourself successfully when you are looking for a job.

Starting Your Own Company

Imagine that you run a company. Give your company a name and decide whether you make products or provide a service. Then choose the types of products or services you offer. You can have any kind of company, but it must be fairly large. Next, imagine you have been asked to help others in your company decide which people to hire—or not hire.

In the following spaces, see how many reasons you can list that could be used either to *screen someone out* or *screen someone in* for hiring. You can list a negative, such as "sloppy appearance," or a positive, such as "good communication skills." Think of at least ten reasons.

_____   _____

_____   _____

_____   _____

_____   _____

_____   _____

_____   _____

_____   _____

_____   _____

After you have done this, go back and check the five reasons you think are the most important.

From the top five, choose the top three reasons and list them here, in order of importance. The most important is number 1.

1. _____

2. _____

3. _____

Good work! You have listed reasons a real employer will use in deciding who to hire. Keep in mind that different employers have different opinions about what is most important. Jobs, too, have varying requirements, depending on what that employee will do.

What Employers Look For

Studies have been made to find out what employers look for in a good employee. Check your list against the findings of these studies.

Employers consider:
- Appearance
- Dependability
- Skills, experience, and training

Let's look at why this is true.

Appearance

This is important because a negative first impression is very hard to change. Employers in one survey said that over 40% of the people they interviewed had a poor appearance. Many employers rejected job seekers because of how they looked. It may not be fair, but it is a fact.

Did you put appearance in your list? _____

Why or why not? _____

_____

Dependability

Most employers will not hire someone they can't count on. How do they decide who they can depend on? They look at the information you provide about previous jobs, school, personal, and other history.

Being *dependable* means being on time, having good attendance, working hard to meet deadlines, and not leaving the job after only a short time. If you convince an employer that you are dependable and hard-working, you will get the job over an equally skilled person who does not.

Did you put dependability on your list? _____

Why or why not? _____

_____

Skills, Experience, and Training

Most employers will interview only those people who meet the minimum requirements for a job. But employers often will hire a person with less experience or training than another applicant. Why? Because they are convinced that person will work harder or be more reliable.

In fact, most decisions are not based only on skills. If the employer thinks you can do the work—or that you can learn to do it quickly—you may get the job. If the employer thinks you will fit right in, be dependable, and work hard, you may get the job over those with more experience than you have!

Did you put Skills, Experience, and Training on your list?_____

Why or why not? _____

_____

Which leads me to Farr's #1 rule of job seeking:

**It is not always the most qualified person who gets the job—
it's the best job seeker!**

Employers Are People, Too

Employers are people, just like you. Wouldn't you want to hire people who:
- Look like they could handle the job,
- Appear to be good, dependable workers, and
- Convince you that they have enough job related skills and training to handle the job—or could learn to quickly?

This is very good news for you because:
- You can learn to create a positive first impression.
- You can emphasize why you can be counted on as a dependable worker.
- You can present your strengths so that you convince an employer that you can do the job.

It is often the most *prepared* job seeker who gets the job, not the best qualified.

This book will help you prepare. You can decide what job you can do well and enjoy. And you will see how to get that job, even over more experienced workers.

2

YOU AND THE 21ST CENTURY

Preparing for Career Growth

Our economy is changing very fast. And no one is sure exactly what this might mean for people who work. As a worker, your ability to adapt to changes will become more and more important to your success. For example, the U. S. Department of Labor estimates that half of all existing jobs will be eliminated in the next 20 years.

Many of these jobs will be replaced by new ones. And people will have to learn to do the new ones. Those who can't or won't will have to take lower paying jobs or stay unemployed. All this could sound discouraging. But the future holds promise if you can accept change and develop the skills you need.

To prepare for the future, you need to think about more than just the type of job you want. You need to consider what is important to you. The better you understand yourself the more successfully you will be able to plan your future.

Each of the following exercises will give you different information about yourself. As you use this book to work on your personal and career plans, you will need this information.

What Do You Want to be Doing in Ten Years?

Imagine yourself ten years from now. Be realistic but positive—it's OK to dream! If you could choose exactly what your life would be like, what would you be doing? Take your time and answer the following questions. Use extra sheets of paper as needed.

1. Where would you be living, in what sort of area, in what sort of home? _____

_____

_____

_____

_____

_____

_____

2. How would you be making a living, doing what sorts of things? _____

_____

_____

_____

_____

_____

3. Who would you be sharing your time with? _____

_____

_____

_____

_____

_____

_____

4. How would you spend your leisure time, doing what sorts of things? _____

_____

_____

_____

_____

_____

5. Any other important details? _____

_____

_____

_____

_____

_____

An Inheritance from Uncle Harry

Let's imagine you just inherited ten million dollars from an uncle you didn't even know you had. (Poor old Uncle Harry.) This means you will never have to work again. But there are a few catches! Harry put the money with a group of people. And these people will give the money to you only after you have met certain conditions. Answer the following questions as honestly as you can.

1. For two years, you will get $60,000 per year for expenses. But you must spend your time learning about something you are interested in. How would you spend this time, doing what?

_____

_____

_____

_____

2. After two years, you must spend half of your money on a project that would help others. What would this project be?

_____

_____

_____

_____

3. What sort of life style would you have after the two years were over? Where would you live, with whom, how would you spend your time?

_____

_____

_____

_____

What Do You Want to Accomplish?

Ten years from now, what are the three things you would like to have accomplished? Don't think of all the reasons you might not succeed. Concentrate on the things you really would like to accomplish.

1. _____

_____

_____

2. _____

_____

_____

3. _____

_____

_____

Making Wishes Come True

Do you have a clear vision of what you want to do in the future? If so, what can you do now to start making your dreams come true? One way is to decide to begin now. Do something now to get you closer to your long-term and seemingly impossible goal.

Look over the exercises you've just completed. Pick the three achievements that seem most important to you and write them here. Be realistic about what you could accomplish if you worked at it. Think in terms of ten years into the future.

1. _____

2. _____

3. _____

For each of these goals, complete the following.

Goal 1:

1. Give details about what you would like to accomplish: _____

_____

_____

_____

_____

2. Think of at least three things you could do in the next two years to come closer to meeting your goal.

a. _____

_____

b. _____

_____

c. _____

_____

3. List at least three things you could do in the next six months to begin working toward this goal.

a. _____

_____

b. _____

_____

c. _____

_____

4. List at least three things you could do in the next 30 days to begin working toward this goal.

a. _____

_____

b. _____

_____

c. _____

_____

Goal 2:

1. Give details about what you would like to accomplish: _____

_____

_____

_____

_____

2. Think of at least three things you could do in the next two years to come closer to meeting your goal.

a. _____

_____

b. _____

_____

c. _____

_____

3. List at least three things you could do in the next six months to begin working toward this goal.

a. _____

_____

b. _____

_____

c. _____

_____

4. List at least three things you could do in the next 30 days to begin working toward this goal.

a. _____

_____

b. _____

_____

c. _____

_____

Goal 3:

1. Give details about what you would like to accomplish: _____

_____

_____

_____

_____

2. Think of at least three things you could do in the next two years to come closer to meeting your goal.

a. _____

_____

b. _____

_____

c. _____

_____

3. List at least three things you could do in the next six months to begin working toward this goal.

a. _____

_____

b. _____

_____

c. _____

_____

4. List at least three things you could do in the next 30 days to begin working toward this goal.

a. _____

_____

b. _____

_____

c. _____

_____

These activities help you understand what goals in your life are worth working for. Include these goals in your career planning. Then you can create a more meaningful and enjoyable future for yourself.

WHAT ARE YOU GOOD AT?

Developing Your Skills Language

Everyone is good at something. In fact, most people are good at many things and don't give themselves credit for them. You may take for granted many things you do well that others would find hard or even impossible to do.

Knowing what you do best is important when you're deciding what kind of work is right for you. It makes a lot of sense to do the things you do best. If you do, you will probably be more successful.

It is also important to do things you enjoy doing. If you enjoy what you do and you're good at it, too, your life will be more satisfying.

This chapter provides a series of exercises to help you identify what you are good at and what you enjoy doing. When you're making important decisions about the careers and jobs you will choose in the future, you can use this knowledge.

Three Types of Skills

Although you have hundreds of skills, you may find it hard to name them. One way to define your skills is to organize them into three groups:

Job Skills: These are skills you need for a specific job. An auto mechanic, for example, needs to know how to tune-up engines, repair brakes, and so on.

Adaptive Skills: These are often defined as personality or personal characteristics. They help a person to adapt to or get along in a new situation. For example, honesty and enthusiasm are traits employers look for in a good worker.

Transferable Skills: These are skills you can use in many different jobs. You can transfer them from one job to a very different one. Writing clearly, for instance, is a skill you can use in almost any job.

It is important that you know what skills you have. Most job seekers think job-related skills are their most important skills. They are important. But employers often select job seekers with less experience because of their adaptive or transferable skills. For this reason, you need to identify your adaptive and transferable skills.

On the following lines, list five traits you have that make you a good worker. Take your time. Think about what an employer might like about you or the way you work.

1. _____

_____

2. _____

_____

3. _____

_____

4. _____

_____

5. _____

_____

Save this list! It can be very important to you! These are your key personality traits. Employers will find them very important in deciding to hire you over someone else. In Chapters Eight, Nine, and Ten, you learn how mentioning these traits will help you in your job search.

Adaptive Skills

You may have overlooked some important skills. The following check list shows skills most employers find important.

Check column one if you have that trait and use or show it in most situations. Check column two if you have the trait but use it or show it only some of the time. Don't mark either column if you use that trait infrequently.

Critical Skills

These are skills all employers value highly. They often won't hire a person who does not have or use some of these.

Employers value people who:	Most of the time	Some of the time		Most of the time	Some of the time
get to work every day			get along well with co-workers		
arrive on time			are honest		
get things done			work hard		
follow instructions from supervisor					

Other Adaptive Skills

Good workers have the following adaptive skills:

	Most of the time	Some of the time		Most of the time	Some of the time
			highly motivated		
			intelligence		
			creativity		
			leadership		
ambition			enthusiasm		
patience			persistence		
assertiveness			self-motivation		
learns quickly			results oriented		
flexibility			pride in doing a good job		
maturity			willingness to learn new things		
dependability			takes responsibility		
completes assignments			asks questions		
sincerity			other:		
problem solving					
friendliness					
a good sense of humor					
physical strength					
good sense of direction					

On the blank lines, add any of your similar traits from the good worker exercise earlier in this chapter. Also add any other personality traits you think are important.

Choose five traits you checked in column 1 that you think are most important to an employer. List them here.

_____

_____

_____

These are the personality traits you should mention in job interviews. For you, these are some of the most important words in this book!

Transferable Skills

The following list contains transferable skills. Go over the list twice. In the first column, check each skill you are strong in. Check column 2 if you want to use this skill in your next job. When you're finished, you should have checked ten to twenty skills in both columns.

Critical Skills

These skills tend to get you higher levels of responsibility and pay. They are worth emphasizing in an interview! If you have these transferable skills, you are able to:

	Strong Skill	Next Job		Strong Skill	Next Job
meet deadlines			solve problems		
speak in public			plan		
supervise others			understand and control budgets		
accept responsibility			increase sales or efficiency		

Other Transferable Skills

	Strong Skill	Next Job		Strong Skill	Next Job
Key Skills			record facts		
instructing others			research		
managing money, budgets			synthesize		
managing people			take inventory		
meeting deadlines			**Working with People**		
meeting the public			administer		
negotiating			care for		
organizing/managing projects			confront others		
public speaking			counsel people		
written communication skills			demonstrate		
Using My Hands/Dealing with Things			diplomatic		
assemble things			help others		
build things			insight		
construct/repair buildings			instruct		
drive, operate vehicles			interview people		
good with hands			kind		
observe/inspect			listen		
operating tools, machines			mentoring		
repair things			negotiate		
use complex equipment			outgoing		
Dealing with Data			patient		
analyze data			persuade		
audit records			pleasant		
budgeting			sensitive		
calculate/compute			sociable		
check for accuracy			supervise		
classify things			tactful		
compare			teaching		
compile			tolerant		
count			tough		
detail-oriented			trusting		
evaluate			understanding		
investigate			**Using Words, Ideas**		
keep financial records			articulate		
locate answers, information			communicate verbally		
manage money			correspond with others		
observe/inspect			create new ideas		
			design		
			edit		

Other Transferable Skills (cont)

	Strong Skill	Next Job
ingenious		
inventive		
library research		
logical		
public speaking		
remembering information		
write clearly		
Leadership		
arrange social functions		
competitive		
decisive		
delegate		
direct others		
explain things to others		
influence others		
initiate new tasks		
make decisions		
manage or direct others		
mediate problems		
motivate people		

	Strong Skill	Next Job
negotiate agreements		
planning		
results oriented		
risk taker		
run meetings		
self-confident		
self-motivated		
solve problems		
Creative/Artistic		
artistic		
drawing, art		
expressive		
perform, act		
present artistic ideas		
dance, body movement		
Other:		

Select the top five skills you want to use in your next job and list them in the following spaces.

1. _____
2. _____
3. _____
4. _____
5. _____

Your Power Skills

You have done some things that have given you a great sense of accomplishment. These could be something you did long ago—or yesterday—that wouldn't mean much to anyone else. Perhaps it was that first bike ride you made all by ourself. Or the delicious bread you baked last week. You may or may not have gotten any recognition for what you did. But you did it well and enjoyed doing it.

Riding a bike requires working independently, persisting until you master the skill, and using your own initiative. To bake bread, you needed to follow directions, organize and measure ingredients, and work with your hands.

These skills are *power skills.* They are transferable skills you are very good at and enjoy using. If you can identify them—and use them in your next job—you have a much better chance of success and satisfaction in your career.

To help identify these skills, complete the following exercises.

1. List three accomplishments that are important to you from the years before high school.

a. _____

_____

b. _____

_____

c. _____

_____

2. List three accomplishments from your high school years.

a. _____

_____

b. _____

_____

c. _____

_____

3. List three accomplishments from your adult years.

a. _____

_____

b. _____

_____

c. _____

_____

4. Select one accomplishment from each group. This should be the one that means the most to you, one you truly enjoyed doing. Write a detailed story about each accomplishment on the following lines. Use your own paper if you need more space.

Story 1: _____

_____

_____

_____

_____

_____

_____

_____

_____

_____

_____

_____

_____

Story 2: _____

Story 3: _____

5. Carefully review each story and circle the skills you mentioned. List these skills in the following spaces. Also, add any skills you must have used or needed—even if you didn't mention them in your stories.

_____	_____
_____	_____
_____	_____
_____	_____
_____	_____
_____	_____
_____	_____
_____	_____

6. Now review your top ten transferable skills. If any skills from that list are not on the list you just made, add them now. Use an extra sheet if necessary. From this combined list, select the five skills you would most enjoy using in your next job.

a. _____

b. _____

c. _____

d. _____

e. _____

These are your *power skills.* You are likely to enjoy and do well in any job that allows you to use all or most of these skills. As one last step, list your five power skills in order of their importance to you.

a. _____

b. _____

c. _____

d. _____

e. _____

The best job for you is one that allows you to do what you enjoy doing and are good at. Most employers believe this, too. They know you will probably succeed in a job you like and do well. So look for jobs that need the skills you are strong in and like to use. If you tell an employer about these skills in an interview, you are more likely to get hired for this kind of job, too!

PLANNING
YOUR CAREER

Selecting a Job Objective

There are about 20,000 job titles in the most recent list from the U. S. Department of Labor. Too many jobs to learn about here! And you may already have a good idea of the type of job you want. Still, there are many similar jobs—using similar skills—you probably haven't considered.

This chapter helps you decide what types of jobs interest you. If you already have a good idea about the job you want, you can learn more about it.

Choosing Your Career

Choosing the right career is not easy. Many people make mistakes. They may even get additional education or training only to find out later that they don't like the career they prepared for. Many others just drop into their jobs. They simply take the first job they're offered.

This section will help you in several ways:

By looking at your interests: You have some idea of the kinds of jobs that interest you. These are often jobs you could do well. Trust your own sense.

By matching what you want with what the job offers: You don't always know what working in a particular job is really like. So you need to define what you want in a job. Then you can see how various jobs match up.

By learning about job titles and similar occupations: There are many jobs you may not consider because you don't know much about them. This section introduces you to new job titles and tells you about them.

By knowing sources of additional information: This chapter contains some information on hundreds of job titles. But once you've decided what jobs you're interested in, it's worth your time to learn more about them. This chapter lists major sources of information about these and many other jobs.

Choosing a Job

Complete the following exercises to learn more about what you want in a job. Then check the Job Matching Chart to see which careers might suit you best.

Job Requirements

One way to narrow down the jobs you might consider is to look at what they require. All jobs require certain skills and qualities. The more important ones are listed here. Check the **Yes** column if you want this item in your next job. Check the **No** column if you don't. If that item is not important to you either way, check the **OK** column.

Skills		**Yes**	**OK**	**No**

Leadership
   Direct others. Skills include organizing, persuading, and supervising.
   Examples: supervisor, chief mechanic, head cashier, office manager, travel guide.

Helping Others
   Help other people. Skills include teaching, counseling, understanding, being patient.
   Examples: teacher, social worker, nurse, paramedic.

Creativity
   Develop new ideas. Skills include designing, inventing, drawing, writing, developing ideas or programs.
   Examples: engineer, dancer, actor, writer, photographer, floral arranger.

Manual Dexterity
   Make, build, fix, or do things. Skills include using machines, tools, and other equipment.
   Examples: mechanic, baker, truck driver, plumber, assembler, dancer, athlete.

Working with Data
   Work with technical information, numbers, written materials.
   Examples: drafter, bookkeeper, land surveyor, dietitian, sanitarian.

Using Words, Ideas
   Use words to show ideas, communicate clearly. Skills include writing, speaking, remembering information, and being creative.
   Examples: writer, editor, politician, correspondence clerk, journalist.

Initiative
   Independently decide what needs to be done. Motivated to do it without close supervision.
   Examples: lawyer, photojournalist, writer, electrician, plumber.

Environment

Geographic Limitations
   Jobs found mostly in certain areas of the country. May require moving.
   Examples: mountain guide, lobster fisherman, coal miner, ski instructor, scuba diver.

Indoors
   Spend work-time inside a specific office or building. May travel to other buildings.
   Examples: salesperson, video game service person, carpet installer, secretary, front desk clerk.

	Yes	OK	No

Outdoors
Spend most of work-time outside. May be limited to a designated area. May include travel.
Examples: line maintainer, meter reader, construction worker, street vendor, zoo caretaker.

Mobility
Have freedom to move about. May or may not be limited to a specific area.
Examples: social worker, mail carrier, firefighter, door-to-door salesperson.

Confinement
Little movement is required. May spend work-time in designated area.
Examples: telephone solicitor, computer operator, dispatcher, receptionist, assembly line worker.

Variety of Tasks
Work-time spent doing lots of different things.
Examples: teacher's aide, police officer, caterer, baby-sitter.

Hazardous
Some danger due to accidents and infection. May be no danger if you follow safety rules.
Examples: construction worker, medical worker, animal trainer, lumber jack.

Physical Stamina
Endure stress and strain on the job. Includes heavy lifting, standing, or being uncomfortable for long periods of time.
Examples: warehouse worker, traffic police officer, firefighter, farm worker, construction worker.

Examining Your Interests

Personal experience plays a large part in forming career interests. Let's examine several sources:

People You Know

The people you know and the jobs they have affect your own ideas. You may not know these people well, but their jobs seem very interesting to you. Write the titles of three such jobs in the following spaces. For each, briefly describe what you like about the job.

Job 1: _____

_____

_____

Job 2: _____

_____

_____

Job 3: _____

_____

_____

Hobbies and Recreational Activities

How do you spend your free time? What are you interested in? What do you know a lot about? Your favorite free-time activities could provide some clues to jobs that might interest you. List these activities and any jobs you can think of that might involve them.

_____

_____

_____

_____

School Subjects and Careers

Take a look at the following list of school subjects and jobs that relate to them. An interest in a subject, even if you did not do well in it, can help you identify possible careers. Circle the subjects and related jobs that appeal to you.

Agriculture: agriculture, forestry, and fishery occupations.

Art: education occupations, performing arts occupations, design occupations, and communication occupations.

Business Education: education occupations, office occupations, service occupations.

Distributive Education: sales occupations.

Driver Education: transportation occupations.

Health: health occupations, scientific and technical occupations.

Home Economics: education occupations, service occupations, social service occupations.

Industrial Arts: agriculture, forestry, and fishery occupations, construction occupations, industrial production occupations, mechanical and repairing occupations, performing arts, design, and communications occupations, scientific and technical occupations, service occupations, transportation occupations.

Language Arts: education occupations, office occupations, performing arts, design, and communications occupations, sales occupations, service occupations, social science occupations, social service occupations.

Mathematics: agriculture, forestry and fishery occupations, construction occupations, health occupations, industrial production occupations, office occupations, performing arts, design, and communications occupations, sales occupations, scientific and technical occupations, social science occupations.

Music: education occupations, performing arts, design, and communications occupations.

Physical Education: construction occupations, education occupations, health occupations, service occupations.

Science: agriculture, forestry, and fishery occupations, education occupations, health occupations, industrial production occupations, office occupations, scientific and technical occupations, social science occupations, transportation occupations.

Social Studies: education occupations, office occupations, performing arts, design, and communications occupations, service occupations, social science occupations, social service occupations.

Some Other Issues

The job matching chart later in this chapter gives information on each of the following issues. Think about how each affects your decision about a career choice.

Future Growth

You should not select a job just because you hear it is a *hot* one. But you can expect some jobs to grow more rapidly than others. These may offer you excellent career opportunities. But even in jobs where little growth is expected, new jobs are opening as employees retire or go on to other jobs.

Earnings

Jobs that require more experience, education, training, or responsibility usually pay better. But some lower paying jobs could allow you to enjoy your work more.

If you're interested in a job you don't qualify for now, don't cross it off your list. Consider an entry level job in the same field. Or get additional training. A lower paying job now may lead to increased earnings in the future.

The job-matching chart uses three categories of earnings, based on 1985 averages:

L = jobs paying below average
M = jobs paying average wages
H = jobs paying high wages

Education and Training

Are you willing to get additional training or education? There are always exceptions, but most jobs require certain levels of training or education.

What is the highest level of education or training you are likely to need for the job you want? Circle the highest level of training or education you would be willing to have for the job you want. The job matching chart uses the same numbers to give the education or training for various jobs.

L = requires high school or less, and the basics usually can be learned in a few months of on-the-job training.

M = requires training after high school such as junior college, an apprenticeship, or requires many years of experience to become qualified.

H = requires four or more years of college

The Job-Matching Chart

The chart that follows provides information on nearly 200 jobs. These are the most popular jobs in the United States, employing over 60% of all workers. The jobs are organized in clusters of similar jobs. Most of the jobs listed are expected to grow rapidly. Some require special training or education.

The columns on the right of each job provide useful information. They cover information you considered in several earlier exercises.

Look over the information on each job. Check the ones you are most interested in. When you are finished, select the top three jobs or top two job clusters. These are the ones you should consider most carefully in your career planning.

If you already know what career you want to enter, the chart will give you additional details.

Job Matching Chart*

Column key

Job requirements: 1. Leadership/persuasion · 2. Helping/instructing others · 3. Problem-solving/creativity · 4. Initiative · 5. Work as part of a team · 6. Frequent public contact · 7. Manual dexterity · 8. Physical stamina

Work environment: 9. Hazardous · 10. Outdoors · 11. Confined · 12. Geographically concentrated · 13. Part-time

Occupational characteristics: 14. Earnings · 15. Employment growth · 16. Number of new jobs through 1995 (in thousands) · 17. Entry requirements

Occupation	1	2	3	4	5	6	7	8	9	10	11	12	13	14	15	16	17
Executive, Administrative, and Managerial Occupations																	
Managers and Administrators																	
Bank officers and managers	•	•	•	•	•	•						•		H	H	119	H
Health services managers	•	•	•	•	•	•								H	H	147	H
Hotel managers and assistants	•	•	•	•	•	•								¹	H	21	M
School principals and assistant principals	•	•	•	•	•	•								H	L	12	H
Management Support Occupations																	
Accountants and auditors		•	•		•	•						•		H	H	307	H
Construction and building inspectors		•	•	•	•		•		•					M	L	4	M
Inspectors and compliance officers, except construction		•	•	•	•		•		•					H	L	10	M
Personnel, training, and labor relations specialists	•	•	•	•	•	•								H	M	34	H
Purchasing agents	•		•		•	•								H	M	36	H
Underwriters			•											H	H	17	H
Wholesale and retail buyers	•	•	•	•	•									M	M	28	H
Engineers, Surveyors, and Architects																	
Architects			•	•	•	•	•							H	H	25	H
Surveyors	•			•			•	•		•				M	M	6	M
Engineers																	
Aerospace engineers			•	•	•							•		H	H	14	H
Chemical engineers			•	•	•									H	H	13	H
Civil engineers			•	•	•									H	H	46	H
Electrical and electronics engineers			•	•	•									H	H	206	H
Industrial engineers			•	•	•									H	H	37	H
Mechanical engineers			•	•	•									H	H	81	H
Metallurgical, ceramics, and materials engineers			•	•	•									H	H	4	H
Mining engineers			•	•	•									H	L	²	H
Nuclear engineers			•	•	•									H	L	1	H
Petroleum engineers			•	•	•							•		H	M	4	H
Natural Scientists and Mathematicians																	
Computer and Mathematical Occupations																	
Actuaries			•	•								•	•	H	H	4	H
Computer systems analysts	•	•	•	•	•							•		H	H	212	H
Mathematicians			•	•										H	M	4	H
Statisticians			•	•										H	M	4	H

¹ Estimates not available.
² Less than 500.

*Reprinted from the *Occupational Outlook Quarterly*, Fall 1986. U.S. Department of Labor Bureau of Labor Statistics.

Job Matching Chart continued

	1. Leadership/persuasion	2. Helping/instructing others	3. Problem-solving/creativity	4. Initiative	5. Work as part of a team	6. Frequent public contact	7. Manual dexterity	8. Physical stamina	9. Hazardous	10. Outdoors	11. Confined	12. Geographically concentrated	13. Part-time	14. Earnings	15. Employment growth	16. Number of new jobs through 1995 (in thousands)	17. Entry requirements
Physical Scientists			●	●										H	M		H
Chemists			●	●										H	L	9	H
Geologists and geophysicists			●	●	●					●		●		H	M	7	H
Meteorologists			●	●	●									H	M	1	H
Physicists and astronomers			●	●										H	L	2	H
Life Scientists																	
Agricultural scientists			●	●										¹	M	3	H
Biological scientists			●	●										H	M	10	H
Foresters and conservation scientists		●	●	●	●			●	●	●				H	L	2	H
Social Scientists, Social Workers, Religious Workers, and Lawyers																	
Lawyers	●	●	●	●	●	●								H	H	174	H
Social Scientists and Urban Planners																	
Economists			●	●										H	M	7	H
Psychologists		●	●	●		●								H	H	21	H
Sociologists			●	●		●								H	L	²	H
Urban and regional planners	●		●	●	●	●								H	L	2	H
Social and Recreation Workers																	
Social workers	●	●	●	●	●	●								M	H	75	H
Recreation workers	●	●	●	●	●	●	●	●		●			●	L	H	26	M
Religious Workers																	
Protestant ministers	●	●	●	●	●	●								L	¹	¹	H
Rabbis	●	●	●	●	●	●								H	¹	¹	H
Roman Catholic priests	●	●	●	●	●	●								L	¹	¹	H
Teachers, Counselors, Librarians, and Archivists																	
Kindergarten and elementary school teachers	●	●	●	●	●	●	●	●						M	H	281	H
Secondary school teachers	●	●	●	●	●	●		●						M	L	48	H
Adult and vocational education teachers	●	●	●	●	●	●	●	●					●	M	M	48	H
College and university faculty	●	●	●	●	●	●		●					●	H	L	−77	H
Counselors	●	●	●	●	●	●								M	M	29	H
Librarians	●	●	●	●	●	●		●					●	M	L	16	H
Archivists and curators			●	●	●									M	L	1	H
Health Diagnosing and Treating Practitioners																	
Chiropractors	●	●	●	●	●	●	●							H	H	9	H
Dentists	●	●	●	●	●	●	●							H	H	39	H
Optometrists	●	●	●	●	●	●	●							H	H	8	H
Physicians	●	●	●	●	●	●	●						●	H	H	109	H
Podiatrists	●	●	●	●	●	●	●							H	H	4	H
Veterinarians	●	●	●	●	●	●	●	●	●					H	H	9	H

¹ Estimates not available.
² Less than 500.

Job Matching Chart continued

Occupation	Job requirements									Work environment				Occupational characteristics			
	1. Leadership/persuasion	2. Helping/instructing others	3. Problem-solving/creativity	4. Initiative	5. Work as part of a team	6. Frequent public contact	7. Manual dexterity	8. Physical stamina	9. Hazardous	10. Outdoors	11. Confined	12. Geographically concentrated	13. Part-time	14. Earnings	15. Employment growth	16. Number of new jobs through 1995 (in thousands)	17. Entry requirements
Registered Nurses, Pharmacists, Dietitians, Therapists, and Physician Assistants																	
Dietitians and nutritionists	●	●	●	●	●	●								M	H	12	H
Occupational therapists	●	●	●	●	●	●	●	●						¹	H	8	H
Pharmacists	●	●	●	●	●							●		H	L	15	H
Physical therapists	●	●	●	●	●	●	●							M	H	25	H
Physician assistants	●	●	●	●	●	●								M	H	10	M
Recreational therapists	●	●	●	●	●	●	●	●		●				M	H	4	M
Registered nurses	●	●	●	●	●	●	●	●	●				●	M	H	452	M
Respiratory therapists	●	●	●	●	●	●	●							M	H	11	L
Speech pathologists and audiologists	●	●	●	●	●									M	M	8	H
Health Technologists and Technicians																	
Clinical laboratory technologists and technicians		●		●		●					●			L	L	18	²
Dental hygienists		●			●	●	●	●					●	L	H	22	M
Dispensing opticians		●	●	●			●	●						M	H	10	M
Electrocardiograph technicians		●	●		●		●							¹	M	3	M
Electroencephalographic technologists and technicians		●	●		●		●							¹	H	1	M
Emergency medical technicians	●	●	●	●	●	●	●	●	●	●				L	L	3	M
Licensed practical nurses		●			●	●	●	●	●				●	L	M	106	M
Medical record technicians			●								●			L	H	10	M
Radiologic technologists		●		●	●	●		●						L	H	27	M
Surgical technicians		●		●	●	●								L	M	5	M
Writers, Artists, and Entertainers																	
Communications Occupations																	
Public relations specialists	●		●	●	●	●								H	H	30	H
Radio and television announcers and newscasters	●	●		●	●	●						●		L	M	6	H
Reporters and correspondents	●		●	●	●	●								¹	M	13	H
Writers and editors	●		●	●	●							●	●	¹	H	54	H
Visual Arts Occupations																	
Designers			●	●	●		●							H	H	46	H
Graphic and fine artists			●	●			●								H	60 M	
Photographers and camera operators			●	●		●	●						●	M	H	29	M
Performing Arts Occupations																	
Actors, directors, and producers			●	●	●	●	●	●				●	●	L	H	11	M
Dancers and choreographers			●	●	●	●	●	●				●	●	L	H	2	M
Musicians			●	●	●	●	●					●	●	L	M	26	M

¹ Estimates not available.
² Vary, depending on job.

Job Matching Chart continued

Column key

Job requirements:
1. Leadership/persuasion
2. Helping/instructing others
3. Problem-solving/creativity
4. Initiative
5. Work as part of a team
6. Frequent public contact
7. Manual dexterity
8. Physical stamina
9. Hazardous

Work environment:
10. Outdoors
11. Confined
12. Geographically concentrated
13. Part-time

Occupational characteristics:
14. Earnings
15. Employment growth
16. Number of new jobs through 1995 (in thousands)
17. Entry requirements

	1	2	3	4	5	6	7	8	9	10	11	12	13	14	15	16	17
Technologists and Technicians Except Health																	
Engineering and Science Technicians																	
Drafters				●			●					●		M	M	39	M
Electrical and electronics technicians			●	●			●					●		M	H	202	M
Engineering technicians			●	●			●					●		M	H	90	M
Science technicians			●	●			●					●		M	M	40	M
Other technicians																	
Air traffic controllers		●	●	●	●		●					●		H	L	[2]	H
Broadcast technicians			●	●			●					●		M	H	5	M
Computer programmers			●	●								●		H	H	245	H
Legal assistants			[3]	●	[3]									M	H	51	L
Library technicians		●		●	●	●					●			L	L	4	L
Tool programmers, numerical control			●				●		●					M	H	3	M
Marketing and Sales Occupations																	
Cashiers		●				●	●					●	●	L	H	566	L
Insurance sales workers	●	●	●	●		●							●	M	L	34	M
Manufacturers' sales workers	●	●	●	●		●								H	L	51	H
Real estate agents and brokers	●	●	●	●		●				●			●	M	M	52	M
Retail sales workers	●	●		●		●							●	L	M	583	L
Securities and financial services sales workers	●	●	●	●		●							●	H	H	32	H
Travel agents	●	●	●	●		●								[1]	H	32	M
Wholesale trade sales workers	●	●	●	●		●								M	H	369	M
Administrative Support Occupations, Including Clerical																	
Bank tellers				●		●					●		●	L	L	24	L
Bookkeepers and accounting clerks				●							●		●	L	L	118	L
Computer and peripheral equipment operators			●	●		●					●			L	H	143	M
Data entry keyers				●			●				●			L	L	10	L
Mail carriers						●	●	●		●				M	L	8	L
Postal clerks					●	●	●	●			●			M	L	−27	L
Receptionists and information clerks		●		●		●					●		●	L	M	83	L
Reservation and transportation ticket agents and travel clerks		●		●		●					●			M	L	7	L
Secretaries			●	●		●	●							L	L	268	L
Statistical clerks				●							●			L	L	−12	L
Stenographers				●	●	●	●							L	L	−96	L
Teacher aides	●	●			●	●	●	●					●	L	M	88	L
Telephone operators		●				●					●			L	M	89	L
Traffic, shipping, and receiving clerks			●	●	●									L	L	61	L
Typists							●				●		●	L	L	11	L

¹ Estimates not available.
² Less than 500.

Column key:

1. Leadership/persuasion
2. Helping/instructing others
3. Problem-solving/creativity
4. Initiative
5. Work as part of a team
6. Frequent public contact
7. Manual dexterity
8. Physical stamina
9. Hazardous
10. Outdoors
11. Confined
12. Geographically concentrated
13. Part-time
14. Earnings
15. Employment growth
16. Number of new jobs through 1995 (in thousands)
17. Entry requirements

Column groups: 1–8 **Job requirements**; 9–13 **Work environment**; 14–17 **Occupational characteristics**

Occupation	1	2	3	4	5	6	7	8	9	10	11	12	13	14	15	16	17
Service Occupations																	
Protective Service Occupations																	
Correction officers	●	●			●		●	●		●				M	H	45	L
Firefighting occupations		●	●	●	●	●	●	●	●				●	M	M	48	L
Guards					●	●	●	●		●			●	L	H	188	L
Police and detectives	●	●	●	●	●	●	●	●	●	●	●			M	M	66	L
Food and Beverage Preparation and Service Occupations																	
Bartenders			●		●	●	●				●		●	L	H	112	M
Chefs and cooks except short order			●			●	●				●		●	L	H	210	M
Waiters and waitresses			●		●	●	●						●	L	H	424	L
Health Service Occupations																	
Dental assistants		●			●	●	●	●					●	L	H	48	L
Medical assistants		●			●	●	●		●					L	H	79	L
Nursing aides		●			●	●	●	●	●				●	L	H	348	L
Psychiatric aides		●			●	●		●	●					L	L	5	L
Cleaning Service Occupations																	
Janitors and cleaners								●					●	L	M	443	L
Personal Service Occupations																	
Barbers					●	●	●				●		●	L	L	4	M
Childcare workers	●	●		●		●		●					●	L	L	55	L
Cosmetologists and related workers					●	●	●	●			●		●	L	H	150	M
Flight attendants		●			●	●	●	●						M	H	13	L
Agricultural, Forestry, and Fishing Occupations																	
Farm operators and managers	●	●	●	●	●		●	●		●				M	L	−62	L
Mechanics and Repairers																	
Vehicle and Mobile Equipment Mechanics and Repairers																	
Aircraft mechanics and engine specialists		●		●		●	●	●	●			●		H	M	18	M
Automotive and motorcycle mechanics		●			●	●	●	●		●				M	H	185	M
Automotive body repairers		●				●	●	●		●				M	M	32	M
Diesel mechanics		●			●	●	●	●		●				M	H	48	M
Farm equipment mechanics		●				●	●	●	●					M	L	2	M
Mobile heavy equipment mechanics		●				●	●	●		●				M	M	12	M

Job Matching Chart continued

	1. Leadership/persuasion	2. Helping/instructing others	3. Problem-solving/creativity	4. Initiative	5. Work as part of a team	6. Frequent public contact	7. Manual dexterity	8. Physical stamina	9. Hazardous	10. Outdoors	11. Confined	12. Geographically concentrated	13. Part-time	14. Earnings	15. Employment growth	16. Number of new jobs through 1995 (in thousands)	17. Entry requirements
Electrical and Electronic Equipment Repairers																	
Commercial and electronic equipment repairers		●	●		●	●								L	M	8	M
Communications equipment mechanics		●	●		●	●								M	L	3	M
Computer service technicians		●	●		●	●								M	H	28	M
Electronic home entertainment equipment repairers		●	●		●	●	●						●	M	M	7	M
Home appliance and power tool repairers		●	●		●	●								L	M	9	M
Line installers and cable splicers		●		●		●	●	●	●					M	M	24	L
Telephone installers and repairers		●		●	●	●	●	●						M	L	−19	L
Other Mechanics and Repairers																	
General maintenance mechanics		●			●		●							M	M	137	M
Heating, air-conditioning, and refrigeration mechanics		●			●		●							M	M	29	M
Industrial machinery repairers		●			●	●	●							M	L	34	M
Millwrights		●			●		●							H	L	6	M
Musical instrument repairers and tuners					●									L	L	1	M
Office machine and cash register servicers		●	●	●		●								M	H	16	M
Vending machine servicers and repairers		●	●			●								¹	M	5	M
Construction and Extractive Occupations																	
Construction Occupations																	
Bricklayers and stonemasons		●		●		●	●	●	●					M	M	15	M
Carpenters		●		●		●	●	●	●					M	M	101	M
Carpet installers		●		●	●	●	●	●						M	M	11	M
Concrete masons and terrazzo workers		●		●		●	●	●	●					M	M	17	M
Drywall workers and lathers		●		●		●	●	●						M	M	11	M
Electricians		●		●		●	●	●	●					H	M	88	M
Glaziers		●		●		●	●	●	●					M	H	8	M
Insulation workers		●		●		●	●	●						M	M	7	M
Painters and paperhangers		●		●	●	●	●	●	●					M	L	17	M
Plasterers		●		●		●	●	●				●		M	L	1	M
Plumbers and pipefitters		●		●	●	●	●	●	●					H	M	61	M
Roofers		●		●		●	●	●	●					L	M	16	M
Sheet-metal workers		●		●		●	●	●						M	M	16	M
Structural and reinforcing metal workers		●		●		●	●	●	●					H	M	16	M
Tilesetters		●		●		●	●							M	M	3	M
Extractive Occupations																	
Roustabouts				●		●	●	●	●			●		M	L	²	L

¹ Estimates not available.
² Less than 500.

Job Matching Chart continued

Column key (Job requirements / Work environment / Occupational characteristics):

1. Leadership/persuasion
2. Helping/instructing others
3. Problem-solving/creativity
4. Initiative
5. Work as part of a team
6. Frequent public contact
7. Manual dexterity
8. Physical stamina
9. Hazardous
10. Outdoors
11. Confined
12. Geographically concentrated
13. Part-time
14. Earnings
15. Employment growth
16. Number of new jobs through 1995 (in thousands)
17. Entry requirements

Occupation	1	2	3	4	5	6	7	8	9	10	11	12	13	14	15	16	17
Production Occupations																	
Blue-collar worker supervisors	●	●	●	●	●		●		●					M	L	85	M
Precision Production Occupations																	
Boilermakers			●				●		●					M	L	4	M
Bookbinding workers		●		●			●	●			●			L	M	14	M
Butchers and meatcutters						●	●	●	●		●			L	L	−9	M
Compositors and typesetters							●	●	●		●			L	M	14	M
Dental laboratory technicians							●				●			L	M	10	M
Jewelers	●	●	●	●	●	●	●				●	●		L	L	3	M
Lithographic and photoengraving workers		●	●	●			●	●			●			H	M	13	M
Machinists			●				●	●	●		●			M	L	37	M
Photographic process workers							●				●			L	H	14	L
Shoe and leather workers and repairers		●			●	●	●							L	L	−8	M
Tool-and-die makers			●				●	●	●		●	●		H	L	16	M
Upholsterers							●	●			●			L	L	6	M
Plant and System Operators																	
Stationary engineers			●				●	●	●					M	L	4	M
Water and sewage treatment plant operators			●	●			●		●	●				L	M	10	M
Machine Operators, Tenders, and Setup Workers																	
Metalworking and plastic-working machine operators							●	●	●		●	●			L	3	L
Numerical-control machine-tool operators			●				●	●	●		●			M	H	17	M
Printing press operators	●	●		●			●	●	●		●			M	M	26	M
Fabricators, Assemblers, and Handworking Occupations																	
Precision assemblers				●			●	●			●			L	M	66	L
Transportation equipment painters							●	●	●		●			M	M	9	M
Welders and cutters							●	●	●	●				M	M	41	M
Transportation and Material Moving Occupations																	
Aircraft pilots		●	●	●			●				●			H	H	18	M
Busdrivers			●		●	●	●				●		●	M	M	77	M
Construction machinery operators				●			●	●	●	●	●			M	M	32	M
Industrial truck and tractor operators			●				●	●			●			M	L	−46	M
Truckdrivers			●				●	●			●			M	M	428	M
Handlers, Equipment Cleaners, Helpers, and Laborers																	
Construction trades helpers				●			●	●	●	●				L	L	27	L

Where to Get More Information

You can get additional information about these and many other jobs. Here are some of the most helpful sources:

Occupational Outlook Handbook (O.O.H): Published every two years by the U.S. Department of Labor, this book is available in most libraries and schools. All the jobs listed in the Job Matching Chart are described in the O.O.H. If you want more information about any of these jobs, this is the best place to start. You will find one or more well-written pages for each job.

Each page is packed with information on what the job is like: working conditions, employment opportunities, training or education required, future trends in that occupation, average earnings, and more.

Guide to Occupational Exploration (G.O.E.): Also published by the Department of Labor, this book lists over 20,000 job titles. In addition, they are cross-referenced in useful ways. You can look up jobs by industry, types of skills required, or related jobs on the Job Matching Chart.

Dictionary of Occupational Titles (D.O.T.): Another book published by the Department of Labor. This one provides brief descriptions on the 20,000 jobs listed in the G.O.E. It is hard to use but provides lots of information.

Library: Most libraries have books and other resource materials on a variety of careers. Ask the librarian for help in finding information about the jobs that interest you.

People: Ask friends, relatives, and others to tell you what they know about the jobs that appeal to you. They also may know about other jobs that would be right for you. Once you get interested in a type of job, find someone who has this kind of job. Ask them what they do or don't like, how they got started, and what advice they can give you about getting a job in that area.

Work in the field: The best way to explore long-term career alternatives is to get a job in that career. Often, you can find entry level jobs that don't require special training. You would then be in a good position to decide to stay there, get additional training, or try something else.

Now you are ready to learn how to find the kinds of jobs you want to do.

TRADITIONAL JOB-HUNTING TECHNIQUES

Some Work Better Than Others

Looking for a job is hard work. If you are lucky, you may find one quickly. But finding even an entry level, minimum wage job can take a long time if you don't know how.

The average adult spends three to five months finding a new job. When unemployment rates are high, you can be out of work even longer. But some people find jobs faster than others, even in times of high unemployment. What do they do differently?

Finding a job takes more than luck. If you use certain methods, you are likely to find a job faster than people who don't. Most of the rest of this book teaches you how to find jobs faster. Better jobs, too!

What Do You Think?

People use many different methods to find jobs. In the following spaces, list as many methods as you can.

_____   _____
_____   _____
_____   _____
_____   _____
_____   _____

Some of these techniques are used by more people than others. (And some of these methods work better than others.) Think about your own experiences and those of people you know. What five job-search techniques do you think most people use to get their jobs? List them here, beginning with the most often used, followed by the second, and so on.

1. _____

2. _____

3. _____

4. _____

5. _____

Brief Review of Traditional Methods

Did you list the traditional methods most job seekers use?

Traditional Methods:

- Filling out applications
- Answering want ads
- Going to the state employment service (sometimes called the *Unemployment Office*)
- Sending out resumes
- Going to private employment agencies

All these methods work for some people. In fact, these techniques are used by most job seekers and many of them do get jobs. But these are not the best methods.

If you cross off these methods from your top five, what is left? If your list includes *personal contacts* or something like it, you are on target. Making personal contacts is one of the most effective methods you can use. Another effective method is making direct contact with an employer—most often after someone has told you that a job may be open.

How People Find Jobs—Facts and Figures

You already know which two job-search methods are most effective, but can you guess how effective? A number of the most often used job-search techniques are listed here, beginning with the most frequently used methods.

Look over the list, then guess what percentage of job seekers used each method to get their jobs. Write the percentage in the first column of the following chart.

What Percentage of Job Seekers Used These Methods to Find Their Jobs?

	Your Guess	Actual
Heard about opening from people I know:	_____	_____
Contacted employer directly:	_____	_____
Answered want ad:	_____	_____
Referred by private employment agency:	_____	_____
Referred by state employment service:	_____	_____
Referred by school placement office:	_____	_____
Took civil service tests:	_____	_____
Other methods:	_____	_____

You can find the correct answers at the end of this chapter. Look them up and enter the correct percentages in the second column.

On the Road to Your Job *(Some ways take longer than others.)*

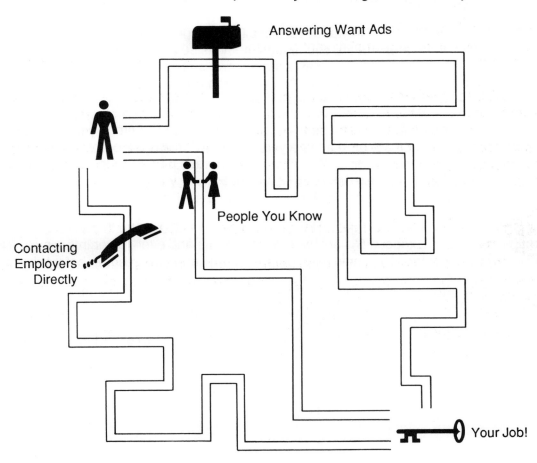

Answering Want Ads

People You Know

Contacting Employers Directly

Your Job!

Traditional and Non-Traditional Job-Seeking Methods

Most people use more than one technique to find job openings. For example, one person might read want ads, fill out applications, and ask friends for leads. Each of these methods works for some people. Other methods are used by other job seekers. Which methods are best for you? Let's look at various job-search methods to find out.

Traditional Job-Search Methods

Traditional job-search methods are not always the most effective ones, but many people do find jobs through them. One or more of these methods can result in your getting a good lead. Here are some frequently used methods, along with some comments on using them effectively.

Want Ads: About 15% of all jobs are advertised in the want ads. This makes want ads worth looking at on a regular basis. There are more ads in the Sunday and Wednesday editions. Look at all the ads. The ones you are interested in may not be listed in an obvious way. A secretarial job could be listed under *General Office* or *Clerical.*

Respond to any ad that sounds interesting, even if you don't have all the qualifications listed. Employers sometimes list things they do not require to limit the response.

Instead of sending in a resume or completing an application, call and ask for the person who supervises the position you want. Ask for an appointment directly, and you are much less likely to be screened out.

Also, look at old want ads. The same organizations may have openings now that have not yet been advertised.

The Employment Service: Only about 5% of all people get their jobs here. Still, it is worth a weekly visit. (In some areas of the country, as many as 30% of all job seekers get job leads from these offices.) There is no fee. The staff sees hundreds of people a week, so ask for the same person each time. If you impress them, they might remember you when they see a good job opening.

Private Employment Agencies: These charge either you or the employer a fee if you get a job through them. It can be 15% or more of a year's wages! Unless the employer pays the fee, this is not a good idea for most people. Watch out for want ads placed by these agencies, too. The advertised job often does not exist, but they will try to refer you to another one paying less money. Only one out of 20 people using an agency gets a job from it. That is a 95% failure rate!

Mailing Resumes: You could get lucky, but resumes sent to no one in particular will probably end up in the trash. Expect a 5% or lower response rate and even fewer interviews. It is almost always better to contact the employer in person. Then send your resume before the interview.

Filling Out Applications: The best time to complete an application is after you have been offered a job. There are times when they are required before an interview, but this is an exception. Many small businesses do not even have applications. It is always better to ask to see the person in charge directly. Fill out an application if you are asked to, but don't expect it to get you an interview.

Volunteering: If you lack experience or are not getting job offers, volunteer to work for free. Perhaps you could offer your services for a day or even a week to show an employer what you can do. Promise that if things don't work out, you will leave with no hard feelings. This really does work, and many employers will give you a chance because they like your attitude.

School Placement Office: If you are lucky enough to have a school counselor or placement staff, get to know them soon. If they have job listings, follow their advice and go to any interviews they set up. Never miss an interview they send you to.

Professional Associations: Many professions have special publications for people who work in that field. They are often a good source of information and some list job openings. Local branches of national organizations sometimes list job openings, too. They are worth checking into.

Civil Service Jobs: Jobs with various government branches are a major part of our labor market. They often require special tests and other procedures. Find out about local, state, and federal jobs by contacting the personnel divisions for each. They are listed in your phone book. It is worth a visit to find out more about how they hire people. But it often takes a long time to get an interview for one of these jobs. And even longer before you get an offer. Even so, they are worth looking into.

Self-Employment: If you want to join the growing number of people who work for themselves, start at the library. There are many helpful books and other resource materials there. Ask the librarian for help! Another good idea is to work in a business like the one you want to start yourself. There is no better way to learn the ropes.

Start at the Bottom: If you are being told you do not have enough experience, take an entry level job in the field you want. Look for ways to work your way up as quickly as possible. Learn as much as you can, let the boss know you want to move up, and take on difficult tasks.

Use the job-seeking methods covered in this chapter. You may find your next job from one of them! But most people find their jobs using other methods. These are covered in Chapter Six.

Answers to How People Find Jobs

The answers are based on a survey of job seekers by the U.S. Department of Labor, Bulletin 1886.

- Heard about opening from people I know: **28.4%**
- Contacted employer directly: **34.9%**
- Answered want ad: **13.9%**
- Referred by private employment agency: **5.6%**
- Referred by state employment service: **5.1%**
- Referred by school placement office: **3%**
- Took civil service tests: **2.1%**
- Other methods: **12%** (examples: union hiring hall; placed ads in journals; went to places where employers come to hire people; and so on.)

THE TWO BEST JOB-SEARCH METHODS

About 70% of All Jobs Are Found Using These

Two job-search methods are more effective than all others put together. This chapter shows you what they are and how to use them.

The Hidden Job Market

Most jobs are not advertised. As you saw in Chapter Five, less than 15% of all people get their jobs through the want ads. Jobs available through private and government employment agencies are also considered public knowledge. Anyone can find out about them.

But these *advertised* openings add up to only about 25% of all job openings. All the rest are hidden from you if you use traditional job-search methods!

Look at the following chart. It shows that only two job-seeking methods—direct contact with employers and getting leads from people you know—are used to find about two-thirds of all jobs.

Using both of these methods, you can find out about unadvertised job openings, where 75% of all jobs are found. For these reasons, most of this chapter emphasizes non-traditional or *informal* job-seeking methods. These are the methods that open doors for you.

How Most Jobs Are Found

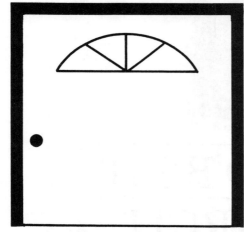   

Direct contact with employers
and leads from people you know
63.3%

Want ads
13.9%

Agencies
12.2%

Others
10.6%

Why Most Jobs Are Not Advertised

Most jobs are never advertised. Why not? Think about this for a bit. Then write three reasons in the following spaces:

1. _____

2. _____

3. _____

Employers don't advertise job openings for many reasons. The most common reasons are:

- They don't like to.
- They often don't need to.

Let's look at each reason.

Employers don't like to advertise: When employers put an ad in the paper, they have to interview all sorts of strangers. Most employers are not trained interviewers and don't enjoy it. They have to interview people who do their best to create a good impression. And they have to eliminate most of them by finding their weaknesses. It's not fun for either side.

Often, employers don't need to advertise: Most jobs are filled before advertising is needed. The employer may already know someone who seems to be right for the job. Or someone hears about the job and gets an interview before it is advertised.

Often, employers hire someone who's been recommended to them by a friend or associate. Employers are much more comfortable hiring a person they know is good rather than someone they don't know at all.

The Four Stages of a Job Opening

If you were depending just on the want ads, you would never know about the good jobs that are not advertised. Someone else would get them.

How to Find Job Openings

But how do you find these openings if they're not advertised? Here is the answer. You have to learn to find employers *before* they advertise the job you want.

To do this, you need to understand how most jobs become available. The opening doors in the following illustration show the four stages of a job opening.

The History of a Job Opening

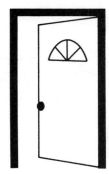
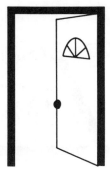

| No job open, but employer meets with you. Afterwards, you send Thank You note and JIST Card. | Need is clear; insiders know. Employer receives follow-up call from you. Is impressed. | Job now open. Employer calls you for second interview. The job is yours! | If you had not contacted the employer, a want ad would have been placed. You and hundreds of others would respond. |

Before a job is filled, a series of events occurs. First, the boss (or someone else in the organization) knows that a job might open up. There is no job then, but a need is beginning to develop. More time passes. The need for the position becomes clear, and a job opening is finally announced. If the job isn't filled, a want ad is placed. Finally, someone is hired.

What Does This Mean to You?

Suppose a friend or relative had given you a name to call in that particular company—just in case there might be a job for you. If you had called the company and made an appointment to talk with them, you would have been using a non-traditional job-search method. And at any point along the line, you might have been a candidate for that job.

For example, at first there is no job, but the employer's door is not completely closed to you. The employer is willing to talk with you about the kinds of jobs available in that type of business. (Most employers will meet with a person recommended to them by someone they know.) After your meeting, you send a thank you note and a JIST Card (Read about JIST Cards in Chapter Eight.) You also promise to call back from time to time.

Later, a need has been recognized and the employer remembers you because you have kept in touch. The door opens a little more.

The job becomes officially open. The employer feels confident about you and your skills. You have demonstrated follow through and you were recommended by an associate. No need for a want ad. The door opens wide. You are hired!

You must develop job-seeking skills that help you see an employer during the early stages of a job opening. Before it is advertised. And in many cases, before there is even an opening.

Small Organizations—Where the Jobs Are

About two-thirds of all workers work in small organizations. Most of the new jobs in our economy now come from small organizations. And the opportunities there are often better than in large companies. Look at the following chart to see the importance of small organizations in your job search.

Where People Work

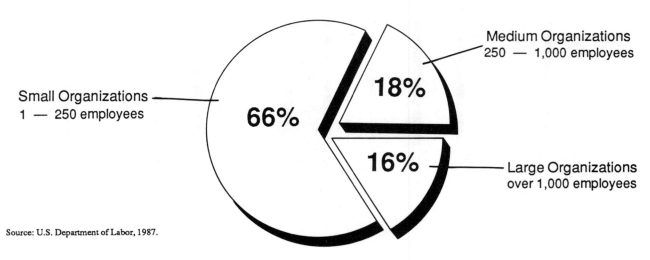

Small Organizations
1 — 250 employees

66%

Medium Organizations
250 — 1,000 employees

18%

16%

Large Organizations
over 1,000 employees

Source: U.S. Department of Labor, 1987.

Many of the non-traditional methods presented in this chapter are most effective with smaller employers. This is the way our economy is headed. But the methods also work well with larger, more formal organizations, too.

Non-Traditional Methods

You have already learned that non-traditional job-search methods are effective. The following is an overview of these methods and how you can use them.

It is useful to separate non-traditional job-search methods into two categories: *warm contacts* and *cold contacts.* When you ask for help or advice from people you know, you are using warm contacts. When you contact people you don't know, you are talking to cold contacts.

Both methods can be very effective if used properly. Since it is often easier to contact people you know, we will begin with warm contacts.

Warm Contacts—Your Network

A *network* is an informal group of people who have something in common. As a job seeker, your network is made up of all the people who can help you—and the people they know. *Networking* is the process you use in contacting these people. You may be surprised at how many people you can meet this way. Let's look at how this works.

Start with the People You Know

Your friends and relatives are the people who are most willing to help you find a job. And they can provide valuable leads. To see how networking can work for you, begin by writing the names of three friends or relatives on the following lines.

1. _____

2. _____

3. _____

Now let's take the first person on the list as an example. If you asked that person for the names of two people, you would have two new contacts. Your network would look like this:

Beginning Your Network

Referral 1   Someone You Know   Referral 2

If you asked each of them for two names and then continued the process, your network would soon look like this:

Your Network Expands

All these people would make up a network you could contact through just one person.

Incredible Arithmetic

The numbers of people you could contact this way are amazing. In this example, if you kept getting two referrals from each person, you would have 1024 people in your network after only the tenth level. And that is starting with only one person!

Networking is a simple idea and it does work. It helps you meet potential employers you would not find using any other method. These potential employers are a friend of a friend of a friend. And they will be willing to see you for this reason.

More About Networking

Here are additional ways to make your network truly effective.

Your Objectives

You need to have clear objectives before you go out to see someone in your network. Write what you think your objectives should be:

_____

_____

_____

_____

Experience shows that you need to meet the following objectives in each of your networking contacts:

Select good contacts: You can begin networking with anyone who knows people and is willing to talk to you. The people you are then referred to are likely to know even more about the job you want. Each referral will try to be helpful and refer you to someone who knows even more than they do.

Present yourself well: You need to convince the people you see that you have the skills to do a good job. They must like you, too, or it will be very difficult to get them to help you. Tell them what sort of job you are looking for and what skills, experience, and other credentials you have for that job.

Get two referrals: Sometimes the person you talk to knows of an opening for someone like you. But more often, they do not. Your objective is to get the names of two people who could also help you in your job search. The following list gives you tips on getting referrals.

Three essential questions to get referrals:

1. Do you know of anyone who might have a job opening in my field?
2. Do you know of anyone who might know of someone who would?
3. Do you know someone who knows lots of people?

It is unusual to get a no if you ask all three questions. Any time you get a yes, get enough details to contact that person!

Networking Groups

You know many groups of people who can help you. The following chart shows a list of groups that other job searchers have thought of. You probably can think of additional groups who can be part of your network.

Sample Networking Groups

Friends	Neighbors
Relatives	Friends of parents
Former employers	Former co-workers
Classmates	Former classmates
Members of my church	Members of social clubs
Members of sports groups	Friends of parents
My friends' parents	People who sell me things (at the store, insurance, etc.)

People who provide me with services (hair stylist, counselor, mechanic, etc.)
Members of a professional organization I belong to (or could quickly join)

Write your own list of at least ten groups on the following form. Since everyone has friends and most have relatives, they have already been listed on the form. Use our examples for ideas and add others to your list that make sense to you.

My Network List: Groups

Friends
Relatives

_____

Each of the groups you have listed can be used to create a list of names for your network. And these people can give you the names of others to contact.

Friends List

Count your friends. Besides close friends, include everyone who knows you by name and is friendly with you.

Write the number here: _____

The next step is to complete a form for this group. The following is a sample form. Your own list may need more spaces, but for now complete the lines available in the sample form.

Networking List—Friends

Name	Phone Number
1.	
2.	
3.	
4.	
5.	

If you do the same thing for each of the groups on your list, you could end up with hundreds of names. Each one of these people knows other people. They would refer you to them if you asked. Then you would have many, many people in your job-search network!

Cold Contacts

Contacting people you don't know is called *cold* contacting. The most common methods are calling an organization without a referral or dropping in without an appointment. Both of these methods are covered here.

Using the Yellow Pages to Make Cold Contacts

In any community, the very best list of organizations that might hire you is the Yellow Pages of the phone book. It lists types of organizations all together by category.

This an easy way to find potential employers. And the telephone is an ideal way to contact these organizations. In one hour, you could call 10 to 20 employers. With the right approach, you could set up one or more interviews in just that short period of time.

What types of organizations would be interested in a person with your skills? Think of the types of Yellow Pages' listings you might find for these employers. Write at least five categories or types of organizations.

1. _____
2. _____
3. _____
4. _____
5. _____

Developing a Prospects List

Use the Yellow Pages to develop a long list of organizations that might need a person with your skills. Here's what you do:

Look through the Yellow Pages' index. For each type of organization, ask "Could this type of organization use a person with my skills?" If the answer is yes, check that type of organization and keep going. After you have gone through all the listings, write the ones you checked on a piece of paper.

Take a look at the following form. This person was looking for a job as a secretary. The form lists Yellow Page headings that could use a person with secretarial skills. In the column on the right, numbers are used to show how interested this person was in working for that type of organization.

General Prospects List

Position desired: _Secretary_

Types of Target Organizations	Level of interest*
1. Advertising	1
2. Airlines	2
3. Attorneys	2

4. _Hospitals_	3
5. _Physicians_	2
6. _Insurance Companies_	3
7. _Television Stations_	1
8. _Banks_	3
9. _Sales Companies_	1
10. _Utilities_	2

* 1 = very 2 = somewhat 3 = not really, but possible

Next, select one of the types of organizations you've listed and turn to that section of the Yellow Pages. The organizations, their telephone numbers, and addresses are all together there. Call each one and ask to come in for an interview.

Although all this sounds easy, making effective phone calls takes practice. Chapter Nine shows you other ways to use the phone to find job leads.

Other Direct Contacts

If you look for them, there are many chances to make direct contacts with employers during your job search. Managers in many small organizations will see you if you just drop in. Even managers in large organizations will see you if you ask to see the person in charge.

Look for businesses that might use someone with your skills. Drop in and ask to see the person in charge. If this person is busy, ask when you should try again. Then call or go back. Usually, people are willing to see you—even on short notice.

Tell them you are looking for a position and would like to speak with them briefly about your qualifications. If you're told they have no openings, say you would still like to talk about the possibility of future openings.

You can learn more about interviewing skills in Chapters Ten and Eleven.

Follow Up!

One of the most effective job-search methods ever used is following up. Send a thank you note after an interview. Arrange to call back at a certain date and time. Also, send a thank you note after a helpful phone conversation with a member of your network. Stay in touch in a friendly and polite way with everyone on your network list.

In the last two chapters you learned the basic methods of finding a job:
- Use a variety of job-seeking methods.
- Get referrals and job leads from people who know you.
- Always try to make a direct contact with the person who will hire you.
- Follow up!

FILLING OUT
APPLICATIONS

Without Burying Yourself

Most large and some small employers require you to fill out an application when you apply for a job. These forms collect information from you that an employer may need.

Why might an employer ask you to complete an application? List some of the reasons.

1. _____

2. _____

3. _____

4. _____

5. _____

You probably listed several good reasons. But did you list that many employers use the application to screen out unqualified job seekers?

Very often, qualified job seekers are screened out, too. In a busy Personnel Office, your application could be eliminated because it is messy. Perhaps you didn't list enough experience. You may have shown that your last job paid more than the one now open. There are many reasons for rejecting an applicant. You might be able to do that job, but you may never have the chance.

Timing is important, too. Suppose you completed your application last week. If a job opens up today, the person who comes in today will be considered before you are. For these reasons, completing an application is not a good way to be considered for a job. Because large organizations usually require applications though, it is worthwhile to learn how to complete them properly.

Application Tips

Follow directions: *Carefully* read and complete all sections of the application. Follow the directions! If you are asked to *print all responses*, do not write! You can make a negative impression quickly if you don't follow directions.

Be neat: A messy application will be rejected immediately. It will make you look as if you don't care. Carry an erasable pen with you for completing applications. These are available at most department stores. Also, most people respond best to black ink.

Provide only positive information: Do not provide negative information. It will be used to screen you out. Leaving a space blank is better than giving information that will get you screened out.

Use all available space to present positive information: For example, list any unpaid (volunteer) experience in the Work Experience section. List training in high school or the military that relates to the job you want. This is an exception to the earlier advice to follow the application's instructions. Find a place to put this helpful information, even if it is the margin!

Handling Problem Questions

Applications ask some difficult questions. Let's review typical problem questions and ways to handle them.

Gaps in Employment

Employers like a complete history. They will wonder what you did during any times you were not employed. If you have a good reason for a gap in your employment history, be sure to list it. Say "raising children," "returned to school," or "helped uncle get a new business started." If you did anything for money during this time say "self-employed." Give details if they support your job objective.

If the gap was several years ago, simply show the start and finish dates of your employment as complete years. For example, *1986 to 1987* does not show any gap at all.

Felony Convictions

If you were arrested but not convicted, say "No."

Disabilities, Physical, or Emotional Problems

Unless your problem prevents you from doing the job safely, it probably is none of their business. Say "No" in almost all cases.

Reason for Leaving Last Job

Don't say "fired" if you were laid off because of a business slowdown or other good reason. Give the reason. If you didn't leave on the best of terms but didn't do anything illegal, it is often best to list a legitimate excuse. Use something neutral, such as "returned to school" or "decided on a career change."

Too Little Experience

If you don't have much experience for the job you want, emphasize your other strengths. List volunteer work as a job in the work section and leave the wages paid blank. Give more details of related training, education and transferable skills used in other jobs, and so on.

Pay Desired

It is often best to say "open" or "negotiable."

Position Desired

If possible, list a broad career field. For example, say "general office" rather than a specific title, such as "secretary." Titles and duties are rarely the same from place to place.

Too Much or Too Little Education

If you are over-qualified or your credentials are strong but in another field, consider leaving out some of your unrelated education. You may be applying for a job that usually requires advanced training or degree. If you did not graduate, say you "attended" certain institutions. Don't say whether you did or did not graduate.

Let Your Conscience Be Your Guide

It should be clear that you could cross a line and start lying on an application. This is not a good idea. Many employers will fire you if they find out you lied on your application. A better approach is to leave a sensitive question blank. If you have a serious problem that an application would reveal, you'll be better off looking for job openings that don't require an application.

The truth is, an application is more likely to do you harm than good. If you do fill one out, be sure that it is as good as you can make it and has nothing in it that could eliminate you from consideration. More effective job-search methods are covered in Chapter Six.

Sample Applications

The first application contains many errors. Find as many as you can and circle them. Don't make the same mistakes on your own application!

Then, for practice, use a pencil or erasable pen to complete the second blank application. Make sure all your dates, addresses, and other information are correct. When you're done, you can tear out this sample and take it with you on your job search. It will provide all the details you might forget (such as dates and phone numbers).

APPLICATION FOR EMPLOYMENT

PERSONAL DATA

NAME *Johnny* LAST *B.* FIRST *Goode* MIDDLE SOCIAL SECURITY NO. *?*

PRESENT ADDRESS *1953* STREET *Grant* CITY STATE ZIP

TELEPHONE NUMBER *none* HOW LONG HAVE YOU LIVED AT PRESENT ADDRESS? _____

PREVIOUS ADDRESS *In another State* STREET CITY STATE ZIP HOW LONG? *2 month*

POSITIONS APPLIED FOR: *any thing*

WORK SCHEDULE DESIRED: ☑ FULL TIME ☑ PART TIME

IF PART TIME, SPECIFY HOURS DESIRED BY DAY: SUN _____

MON *days* WED _____ FRI →

TUES. _____ THURS. → SAT.

RATE OF PAY EXPECTED: ☑ START *at least $9.* 6 MO. _____ 1 YEAR _____

HOW DID YOU HEAR OF THIS OPENING? *I just walked in to fill out an Application*

HAVE YOU WORKED WITH US BEFORE? ☐ NO ☐ YES – WHEN/HOW LONG? _____

PREVIOUS JOB TITLE *unemployed* REASON FOR LEAVING *boss didn't like me*

LIST ANY FRIENDS/RELATIVES WORKING WITH US NOW *none that I know of*

LIST ANY SPECIAL SKILLS YOU HAVE FOR POSITIONS APPLIED FOR ABOVE _____

☐ ARE YOU OVER 21? ☐ YES ☑ NO (If No, hire is subject to minimum legal age verification.)

☑ SEX: ☐ MALE ☐ FEMALE ☑ HEIGHT: *5* Ft. *2* In. ☐ WEIGHT *2 00* LBS.

☐ MARITAL STATUS: ☐ SINGLE ☐ MARRIED ☐ SEPARATED ☐ DIVORCED ☐ WIDOWED

☐ No. YEARS MARRIED _____ No. of Dependents *just me* (INCLUDE YOURSELF)

☐ HAVE YOU EVER BEEN BONDED? ☐ NO ☐ YES – WHEN *?*

☐ HAVE YOU EVER BEEN CONVICTED OF A CRIME IN THE PAST 10 YEARS (Excluding Traffic Violations)? ☐ No ☐ Yes

IF YES, LIST CONVICTIONS *got picked up at a few parties but it wasn't my fault*

☐ DO YOU HAVE ANY PHYSICAL HANDICAPS PREVENTING YOU FROM DOING CERTAIN TYPES OF WORK? ☐ No ☑ Yes IF YES, DESCRIBE HANDICAP/LIMITATIONS *nerves*

☐ HAVE YOU HAD ANY SERIOUS ILLNESS IN THE PAST 5 YEARS? ☐ NO ☑ YES IF YES, DESCRIBE *Nerves, I'm ok now though*

☑ *I'm in a substance abuse*

LIST IN REVERSE ORDER BEGINNING WITH PRESENT EMPLOYER (1) COMPANY NAME (3) CITY/STATE/ZIP (2) ADDRESS (4) CONTACT & PHONE	POSITION JOB/TITLE	DATES FROM	TO	SALARY BEGINNING	ENDING	REASON FOR LEAVING
1 Don's Rentals	labor	June	Oct	min wage		Didn't pay enough
2 St. Paul						
3						
4 ☑ active machine	fixed	Jan '88	about			the boss didn't like me.
1 repair	broken	July 1988		#6 hr.		
2 Minn, MN	equipment					
3						
4 ☐						didn't like the job. Too dirty.
1						
2						
3						
4 ☐						

REFERENCES:

MAY WE CONTACT THE EMPLOYER AT THE PHONE GIVEN
☐ IF YES ☐ LEAVE BLANK IF NO

BRANCH	RANK	DUTIES	SALARY FROM	TO	REASON FOR CHANGE IN RANK
USN	E2	electronics	—		got busted

LIST ANY SPECIAL SCHOOL OR SKILLS ACQUIRED DURING YOUR MILITARY SERVICE   Radio

NAME	ADDRESS	RELATIONSHIP	PHONE NUMBER
Franny Goode	St. Paul	Mother	none

APPLICANT: READ AND SIGN BELOW

The information provided by me in this application for employment is true and complete to the best of my knowledge. I understand that if I am employed, any false statements will be considered as cause for possible dismissal. You are hereby authorized to conduct any investigation of my personal history and/or credit and financial records employing investigative or credit agencies or bureaus of your choice subject to the provisions of the Fair Credit Reporting Act.

J. B. Goode   2/12/91

SIGNATURE OF APPLICANT   DATE

APPLICANT – DO NOT WRITE IN THIS SECTION

INTERVIEWER	DATE	COMMENTS

DEPARTMENT	POSITION	WILL REPORT	LOCATION	SALARY

APPROVED: PERSONNEL DEPARTMENT	DEPARTMENT MANAGER	GENERAL MANAGER

EDUCATIONAL HISTORY

LIST EDUCATIONAL INSTITUTIONS BELOW — USE DUPLICATES WHERE YOU CHANGED SCHOOLS.

	NAME AND ADDRESS OF SCHOOL	CIRCLE LAST GRADE COMPLETED	GRADUATED	DEGREE/MAJOR GRADE POINT AVERAGE
ELEMENTARY	# 22	6 7 ⑧ 9	☑ YES / ☐ NO	none
JR. HIGH	didn't go to one	7 8 9	☐ YES / ☐ NO	
JR. HIGH		7 8 9	☐ YES / ☐ NO	
HIGH SCHOOL	Central	9 10 ~~11~~ ⑫	☑ YES / ~~☐ NO~~	none C-
HIGH SCHOOL		9 10 11 12	☐ YES / ☐ NO	
COLLEGE	Orange County CC	① 2 3 4	☐ YES / ☑ ~~NO~~	Took some classes there
COLLEGE		1 2 3 4 MASTERS _____ DR._____	☐ YES / ☐ NO	
OTHER	military	☑ YES / ☑ NO		passed electro courses

EXPLAIN ANY SPECIALIZED TRAINING, ADDITIONAL SCHOOLING OR EDUCATIONAL AWARDS I did, OK in
USN ~~and~~ but didn't get any awards

PERSONAL REFERENCES

NAME	ADDRESS	RELATIONSHIP	PHONE NUMBER
Franny Goode	Minn MN		
Aunt Beth	"		

LIST ONLY PERSONS WE MAY CONTACT — BE SURE TO INCLUDE PHONE NUMBER

APPLICATION FOR EMPLOYMENT

PERSONAL DATA

NAME _____ SOCIAL SECURITY NO. _____
LAST   FIRST   MIDDLE

PRESENT ADDRESS _____
STREET   CITY   STATE   ZIP

TELEPHONE NUMBER _____ HOW LONG HAVE YOU LIVED AT PRESENT ADDRESS? _____

PREVIOUS ADDRESS _____ HOW LONG? _____
STREET   CITY   STATE   ZIP

POSITIONS APPLIED FOR: WORK SCHEDULE DESIRED: ☐ FULL TIME ☐ PART TIME

_____   IF PART TIME, SPECIFY HOURS DESIRED BY DAY: SUN _____

_____   MON _____ WED _____ FRI _____

_____   TUES. _____ THURS. _____ SAT. _____

RATE OF PAY EXPECTED: ☐ START _____ 6 MO. _____ 1 YEAR _____

HOW DID YOU HEAR OF THIS OPENING? _____

HAVE YOU WORKED WITH US BEFORE? ☐ NO ☐ YES – WHEN/HOW LONG? _____

PREVIOUS JOB TITLE _____ REASON FOR LEAVING _____

LIST ANY FRIENDS/RELATIVES WORKING WITH US NOW _____

LIST ANY SPECIAL SKILLS YOU HAVE FOR POSITIONS APPLIED FOR ABOVE _____

☐ ARE YOU OVER 21? ☐ YES ☐ NO (If No, hire is subject to minimum legal age verification.)

☐ SEX: ☐ MALE ☐ FEMALE ☐ HEIGHT: _____ Ft. _____ In. ☐ WEIGHT _____ LBS.

☐ MARITAL STATUS: ☐ SINGLE ☐ MARRIED ☐ SEPARATED ☐ DIVORCED ☐ WIDOWED

☐ No. YEARS MARRIED _____ No. of Dependents _____ (INCLUDE YOURSELF)

☐ HAVE YOU EVER BEEN BONDED? ☐ NO ☐ YES – WHEN _____

☐ HAVE YOU EVER BEEN CONVICTED OF A CRIME IN THE PAST 10 YEARS (Excluding Traffic Violations)? ☐ No ☐ Yes

IF YES, LIST CONVICTIONS _____

☐ DO YOU HAVE ANY PHYSICAL HANDICAPS PREVENTING YOU FROM DOING CERTAIN TYPES OF WORK? ☐ No

☐ Yes IF YES, DESCRIBE HANDICAP/LIMITATIONS _____

☐ HAVE YOU HAD ANY SERIOUS ILLNESS IN THE PAST 5 YEARS? ☐ NO ☐ YES IF YES, DESCRIBE

_____

_____

_____

☐ _____

EMPLOYMENT DATA

(1) COMPANY NAME (3) CITY/STATE/ZIP (2) ADDRESS (4) CONTACT & PHONE	POSITION JOB/TITLE	DATES FROM	TO	SALARY BEGINNING	ENDING	REASON FOR LEAVING
1						
2						
3						
4 ☐						
1						
2						
3						
4 ☐						
1						
2						
3						
4 ☐						

REFERENCES:

MAY WE CONTACT THE EMPLOYER AT THE PHONE GIVEN
☐ IF YES ☐ LEAVE BLANK IF NO

MILITARY

BRANCH	RANK	DUTIES	SALARY FROM	TO	REASON FOR CHANGE IN RANK

LIST ANY SPECIAL SCHOOL OR SKILLS ACQUIRED DURING YOUR MILITARY SERVICE _____

PERSONAL REFERENCES

NAME	ADDRESS	RELATIONSHIP	PHONE NUMBER

APPLICANT: READ AND SIGN BELOW

The information provided by me in this application for employment is true and complete to the best of my knowledge. I understand that if I am employed, any false statements will be considered as cause for possible dismissal. You are hereby authorized to conduct any investigation of my personal history and/or credit and financial records employing investigative or credit agencies or bureaus of your choice subject to the provisions of the Fair Credit Reporting Act.

_____

SIGNATURE OF APPLICANT   DATE

APPLICANT – DO NOT WRITE IN THIS SECTION

INTERVIEWS

INTERVIEWER	DATE	COMMENTS

HIRED

DEPARTMENT	POSITION	WILL REPORT	LOCATION	SALARY

APPROVED: PERSONNEL DEPARTMENT	DEPARTMENT MANAGER	GENERAL MANAGER

EDUCATIONAL HISTORY

LIST EDUCATIONAL INSTITUTIONS BELOW — USE DUPLICATES WHERE YOU CHANGED SCHOOLS.

	NAME AND ADDRESS OF SCHOOL	CIRCLE LAST GRADE COMPLETED	GRADUATED	DEGREE/MAJOR GRADE POINT AVERAGE
ELEMENTARY		6 7 8 9	☐ YES ☐ NO	
JR. HIGH		7 8 9	☐ YES ☐ NO	
JR. HIGH		7 8 9	☐ YES ☐ NO	
HIGH SCHOOL		9 10 11 12	☐ YES ☐ NO	
HIGH SCHOOL		9 10 11 12	☐ YES ☐ NO	
COLLEGE		1 2 3 4	☐ YES ☐ NO	
COLLEGE		1 2 3 4 MASTERS _____ DR._____	☐ YES ☐ NO	
OTHER			☐ YES ☐ NO	

EXPLAIN ANY SPECIALIZED TRAINING, ADDITIONAL SCHOOLING OR EDUCATIONAL AWARDS _____

PERSONAL REFERENCES

NAME	ADDRESS	RELATIONSHIP	PHONE NUMBER

LIST ONLY PERSONS WE MAY CONTACT — BE SURE TO INCLUDE PHONE NUMBER

JIST CARDS

Your Personal Calling Card

Imagine that you are an employer and can hire someone for a position in an auto shop. You may or may not have a job opening now. Read the card below, and then answer the questions that follow it.

John Kijek   **home**: (219) 232-9213
                                           message: (219) 637-6643

Position Desired: Auto mechanic

Skills: Over three years work experience including one year in a full-time auto mechanic's training program. Familiar with all hand tools and basic diagnostic equipment. Can handle common auto repair tasks such as tune ups, brakes, exhaust systems, electrical and mechanical repairs. Am a fast worker, often completing jobs correctly in less than the standard time. Have all tools required to start working immediately.

Prefer full-time work, any shift

Honest, reliable, good with people

What Do You Think?

Please answer these questions. Be truthful. Base your answers on your own responses to the information on the card.

1. Do you feel good about this person? (yes or no)_____

2. What were your emotions about this person, how did you feel about him?_____

_____

_____

_____

3. Would you be willing to see him if you had a job opening? (yes or no) _____

Why? _____

_____

_____

4. Would you be willing to see him even if you did not have a job opening? (yes or no)_____

Why? _____

_____

_____

What It Is

This a JIST Card. JIST stands for **J**ob **I**nformation and **S**eeking **T**raining. It is a name used to identify a whole series of job-search techniques I developed in the early 1970s.

Most people can read the example in fewer than 30 seconds. Yet in that very short period of time, the JIST Card creates a positive impression! In fact, most people who read it say they would interview such a person—based on just this much information.

How to Use It

A JIST Card is a 3" x 5" card you can use in many ways like a mini-resume or business calling card. The card is usually printed so that you can have plenty to use during your job search.

Uses for Your JIST Card:

- Attach it to a completed application.
- Give it to a friend or relative. Ask them to keep you in mind if they hear of any job openings. And ask them to give the card to someone else who might know of a job.
- Send one to an employer before an interview.
- Enclose one in your thank you note after an interview or phone contact.
- Give several to people who are willing to give them to others. Besides your friends and relatives, give cards to your insurance person, hairdresser, neighbors, and others who know you.
- Attach one to a resume.

The Parts of a JIST Card

The JIST Card doesn't contain many details, but consider what John Kijek's card does include:

Identification: John's name is given.

A way to contact him: John lists two phone numbers. An employer will almost always call rather than send a letter. By giving the number of a reliable friend who will take messages, John can usually be reached.

Length of experience: John listed his total length of experience. John is a young person looking for his first full-time job. He has had after-school jobs, including one in a fast food restaurant. This is where John developed some skills and learned to be a hard worker. He can describe this experience in the job interview, along with his informal experience working on cars as a hobby.

Related education and training: John listed training with his experience to give a longer total of work and training time. A person with more experience could list training separately.

Skills: This section tells what John can do and how well he can do it. These are job-related skills. John also mentions an important transferable skill—he is fast and thorough in his work.

Preferred working conditions: John has listed two preferences for the type of work he wants. Both of these are positives.

Good worker traits: John lists adaptive traits that would be important to most employers.
   All this in fewer than 30 seconds!

Anatomy of a JIST Card

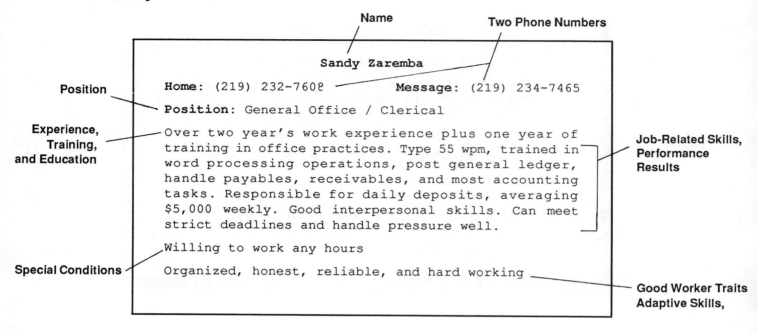

Name

Two Phone Numbers

Position

Experience, Training, and Education

Special Conditions

Job-Related Skills, Performance Results

Good Worker Traits Adaptive Skills,

```
                    Sandy Zaremba

     Home: (219) 232-7608    Message: (219) 234-7465

     Position: General Office / Clerical

     Over two year's work experience plus one year of
     training in office practices. Type 55 wpm, trained in
     word processing operations, post general ledger,
     handle payables, receivables, and most accounting
     tasks. Responsible for daily deposits, averaging
     $5,000 weekly. Good interpersonal skills. Can meet
     strict deadlines and handle pressure well.

     Willing to work any hours

     Organized, honest, reliable, and hard working
```

3" x 5" Pastel Card

Sample JIST Cards

Here are some sample JIST Cards. Study them and use any ideas that help you with your own card.

Dennis Franz   Home: (614) 788-2434
                          Answering Service: (614) 355-0068

Job Objective: Building Maintenance

Skills: Four years plant maintenance experience, meeting safety standards, and maintaining equipment and supply inventories. Supervised sophisticated procedures to maintain "clean rooms." Reorganized workloads so that retiring full-time staff could be replaced by part-time workers from a local Technical Institute. So far this plan has saved the company $22,000. I take pride in operating a safe, sanitary, and efficient building.

Can work any shift

Well-organized, problem-solver, willing to relocate

HOWARD ADAMS-KENNEDY

(205) 663-0953   (205) 791-6610

OBJECTIVE: Administrative

SKILLS: Experienced in administering governmental programs. Set up State Task Force for Environmental Issues. Directed formation and installation of statewide policies for waste disposal and water treatment. Set up a federal pilot project that has been called a national standard for integrating historical preservation and affordable housing. B.S. in Environmental Studies with graduate work in Urban Studies.

Willing to relocate

Creative, aggressive, articulate, able to find common interests among competing groups.

Sandra Benson

(216) 303-7721

(216) 644-2985

Job Objective: Landscaper

Skills: Six years experience in landscaping—mowing, pruning, trimming, and planting. Can drive dump truck and operate heavy machinery. Also skilled in equipment repair. Have own tools. Have taken Community College courses in landscape design and plant care. Enjoy working outside and seeing the results of my efforts.

Full-time work with a company that encourages advancement.

Healthy, energetic, responsible, and efficient.

James Miller

(202) 766-1430   (202) 293-7294

Position Desired: Crane Operator

Skills: Eight years experience with overhead cranes. Can work at extreme heights with no difficulty. Very careful handling materials and following instructions. Perfect safety record and excellent attendance. Able to work well with others.

Available for all shifts

Reliable • Punctual • Honest

THOMAS WELBORN
Home: (602) 253-9678
Leave Message: (602) 257-6643

OBJECTIVE: Electronics—installation, maintenance & sales

SKILLS: Four years work experience plus two years advanced training in electronics. A.S.degree in Electronics Engineering Technology. Managed a $300,000/yr. business while going to school full time, with grades in the top 25%. Familiar with all major electronics diagnostic and repair equipment. Hands on experience with medical, consumer, communications, and industrial electronics equipment and applications. Good problem-solving and communication skills. Customer service oriented.

Willing to do what it takes to get the job done.

Self-motivated, dependable, learn quickly

Deborah Levy
Home: (213) 432-8064
Message: (213) 888-7365

Position Desired: Hotel Management

Skills: Four years experience in sales, catering, and accounting in 300-room hotel. Associate's Degree in Hotel Management plus one year with the Boileau Culinary Institute. Doubled revenues from meetings and conferences. Increased dining room and bar revenues by 44%. Have been commended for improving staff productivity and courtesy. I approach my work with industry, imagination, and creative problem-solving skills.

Enthusiastic, well-organized, detail-oriented.

Sharon Greenwell

Messages: (317) 637-8242

Position Desired: Computer Programmer/Program Maintenance

Knowledge/Skills:

Over five years of combined training and experience in programming. Have written and debugged 45 programs in various languages, including COBOL, BASIC, FORTRAN, and PASCAL. Familiar with IBM, VAX, and Hewlett-Packard computers. Excellent at trouble-shooting and have been praised for my skills in writing documentation.

Prefer daytime shift

Dependable, resourceful, congenial, and meet deadlines.

JIST Card Worksheet

Follow these instructions to create your own JIST Card.

1. Your Name: _____

    Tips: Don't use nicknames or initials if possible.

2. Phone Number: _____

Alternate phone number: _____

    Tips: If you don't have a phone, get permission to use a friend's or relative's. Have a second number to use if you are not at home. Include your area code.

3. Job Objective: _____

    Tips: Don't be too narrow in your job objective. Say "general office" rather than "receptionist" if you would consider a variety of office jobs. If you are more narrow in your job objective, try to avoid a job title but give other details. For example, say "Management position in an insurance related business" or "Working with children in a medical or educational setting."

    Don't limit yourself to entry level jobs if you have potential or interest in doing more. If you say "Office Manager" instead of "secretary," you just might get it. If you are not too sure of your ability to get a higher paying job, it is still best to keep your options open if possible. Say "Office manager or responsible secretarial position," for example.

4. Length of Experience:_____

    Tips: You want to take advantage of *all* the experience you have that supports your job objective. If you are changing careers, have been out of the work world for a while, or do not have very much work experience, you will need to use other experiences to convince the employer you can do the job.

    Some examples include:

Paid Work: You can list any work you were paid to do. The work does not have to be similar to the job you are looking for now. Baby-sitting and lawn-mowing jobs count. So can working in a fast food place. If you worked part time, estimate the number of hours you worked. Divide this total number of hours by 160 (hours) to get the number of months you worked.

Volunteer Work: You can include volunteer work as part of your total. Do this if you don't have very much paid work experience.

Informal Work: Include work you did at home or as an unpaid hobby. It is best if this work relates to the job, but it doesn't have to. For example, if you worked on cars at home and want to be an auto mechanic, there is an obvious connection. You may have experience taking care of younger brothers or sisters. Or working in the family business. Use this experience, too.

Related Education and Training: If you took business courses in high school and want to be an accounting clerk, the courses are part of your experience. So are any courses you took after high school that relate in some way to the job you want.

To figure out your total experience, complete the following table. Write either years or months (if you don't have much experience) in the spaces beside each question.

Your Total Experience Includes:

a. Total of paid work   _____

b. Total of volunteer work   + _____

c. Total of informal work   + _____

d. Total of related education or training   + _____

Total Experience   = _____

Tips for Writing Your Experience Statement

Because everyone has a different background, no single rule can be given for everyone. Here are some tips for writing your own experience statement.

If you have lots of work experience: If part of this experience is not related, you can leave it out. If you have 20 years of experience, say "Over 15" or include just the experience that directly relates to this job. This keeps the employer from knowing how old you are. Your age is an advantage you will present in the interview!

If you don't have much paid work experience: You need to include everything possible. If you have no paid work experience in the field you want to work in, emphasize training and other work. For example, "Nearly two years of experience including one year of advanced training in office procedures."

Remember to include the total of all paid and unpaid work as part of your experience! Include all those part-time jobs by saying "Over 18 months total work experience. . ."

If your experience is in another field: Just mention that you have "Four years work experience" without saying in what.

Other: If you won promotions, raises, or have other special strengths, this is certainly the time to say so. "Over seven years of increasingly responsible work experience, including three years as a supervisor. Promoted twice."

5. Education and Training Statement

Depending on your situation, you can combine your education and training with your experience (as it was in one of the examples just discussed) or list them separately. Don't mention it at all if it doesn't help you. If you have a license, certification, or degree that supports your job objective, you may want to mention it here, too. For example: "Four years of experience plus two years of training leading to certification as an Emergency Medical Technician."

Look over the sample JIST Cards for more ideas and write your own education and training statement here:

_____

_____

_____

_____

_____

6. Skills Section

In this section you list the things you can do. Mention any job-related tools or equipment you can use. Use the language of the job to describe the more important things you can do. It is best to use some numbers to strengthen what you say and emphasize results. Instead of saying "Skills include typing, dictation, (and so on)," say "Type 60 wpm accurately and take dictation at 120 wpm."

Emphasize results: It is too easy to overlook the importance of what you do. Add up the numbers of transactions you handled, the money you were responsible for, the results you got. Some examples:

A person with fast food experience might write "Have handled over 50,000 customer contacts with total sales of over $250,000 quickly and accurately." (These figures are based on a five-day week, 200 customers a day for one year, and an average sale of $5.)

Someone who ran a small store could say "Responsible for business with over $150,000 in sales per year. Increased sales by 35% within 18 months."

Present a successful high school fund-raising project as: "Planned, trained, and supervised a staff of six on a special project. Exceeded income projections by 40%."

Also include one or more of your transferable skills that are important for that job. A receptionist might add "Good appearance and pleasant telephone voice." It is certainly OK to give numbers to support these skills, too! A warehouse manager might say "Well organized and efficient. Have reduced expenses by 20% while orders increased by 55%."

Look over the sample JIST Cards and write your own statement here. _____

_____

_____

_____

_____

_____

_____

_____

_____

_____

7. Preferred Working Conditions

This is an optional section. You can add just a few words— one line at most—to let the employer know what you are willing to do. Do not limit your employment possibilities by saying

"Will only work days" or "No travel wanted." It is better to leave this blank than give anything negative. Look at the sample JIST Cards for ideas. Then write your own statement.

_____

_____

_____

_____

_____

8. Good Worker Traits

List three or four of your adaptive traits. Choose traits that are important in the job you are seeking. Be certain you do have them! The Sample JIST Cards will give you ideas. Then list your own here.

_____

_____

_____

_____

_____

The Final Edit

To fit all this information on a 3" x 5" card, you may need to edit what you've written. Make every word count in your final version. Use short, choppy sentences. Get rid of anything that does not directly support your job objective. Add more information if your JIST Card is too short. Then read your card out loud to see how it sounds. And ask someone else to help you with the final version.

Production Tips

You can type individual JIST Cards—or even hand write them—but it is much better to have them printed. Five copies of the same card can fit on one standard sheet of 8 1/2" x 11" paper. Make sure your final version is error free and typed on a good typewriter. Bring it to a local print shop and have at least a hundred sheets printed. Ask for light card stock in off-white, light buff, or light blue. The cost for printing and cutting the cards should be under $30.

Many print shops can also type or typeset your JIST Cards for an extra fee. It may be worth this to get a professional appearance. Also note that typesetting allows you to put more content on your card if you feel you need to.

Once you have your JIST Cards, use them! Give them away freely because they will not help you get a job if they sit on your desk!

DIALING FOR DOLLARS

Getting Results with Telephone Contacts

Using the telephone is one of the most efficient ways of looking for work. You don't spend any time traveling, and you can talk to large numbers of people in a very short time. In one morning, for example, you can easily talk to more than 20 employers once you learn how.

In fact, many job seekers get more interviews by using the phone than with any other method. You can call people you already know to get interviews or referrals. And you can contact employers whose names you get from the Yellow Pages in the phone book.

This chapter shows you some very effective ways to use the telephone to find job openings and set up interviews.

Overcoming Fear

You may find it hard to use the phone in the way I suggest. Many people do. They think it is "pushy" to call someone and ask for an interview. Before you decide this technique is not for you, think about why you are afraid. What is the worst thing that can happen to you? Most calls take only a minute or so. And most employers don't mind talking to a person they might be interested in hiring.

These calls do require you to overcome some shyness, but they are really quite easy to do. Start with people you know. Then call the people they refer you to. Soon you will find that most people are happy to help you. Even people you just picked from the Yellow Pages will treat you well. The experience of thousands of job seekers is that very few people will be rude to you. And you probably wouldn't want to work for that sort of person anyway.

Sample JIST Card Phone Contact

You can base your phone calls on your JIST Card. Look at the following example to see how one person used their JIST Card to develop a phone call. As you read the call, imagine you are an employer who hires people with these skills. Would you be interested in interviewing this person?

"Hello, My name is John Kijek. I am interested in a position as an auto mechanic. I have over three years of experience, including one year in a full-time auto mechanic's training program. I am familiar with all hand tools and basic diagnostic equipment and can handle common auto repair tasks, such as tune ups, brakes, exhaust systems, electrical and mechanical repairs. I also work quickly, often completing jobs correctly in less than the standard time. I have all the tools needed to start work immediately. I can work any shift and prefer full-time work. I am also honest, reliable and good with people. When may I come in for an interview?"

How Would You Feel?

Before you go on, write how you might feel about a person who called you—an employer—with this approach. If you needed someone like this, would you give him an interview?

_____

_____

_____

Most people say they would give him an interview if they had an opening. Not everyone, but most. For this reason, reading a *JIST script* is a very effective way to use the telephone.

Tips for Completing Your Phone Script

To help you write your script, this chapter shows you a worksheet and tips on how to use it. Read the tips carefully. Then use the information on your JIST Card to help you fill in each section of your script. Work with a pencil so that you can rewrite or make changes easily.

Write exactly what you will say on the phone: A script will help you present yourself effectively and keep you from stumbling around for the right word.

Keep your telephone script short: Just present the information an employer would want to know about you and ask for an interview.

Write your script the way you talk: Since you have already completed your JIST Card, use it as the basis for your telephone script. Your JIST Card uses short sentences and phrases, and you probably wouldn't talk that way. So add some words to your script to make it sound natural when you say say it out loud.

Anatomy of a Phone Script

Your script is divided into the following five sections:

Your Name

This one is easy. All you have to do is fill in the blank on your worksheet.

Your Objective

Always begin your statement with "I am interested in a position as. . .". This approach works! For example, if you say "Do you have any jobs?" the person you are talking to will often say "No."

It takes you only about 30 seconds to read your phone script, and you don't want to get rejected before you begin! So don't use the word *job* in your first sentence. If you say you are "looking for a job" or anything similar, you will often be interrupted. Then you will be told there are no openings.

If the job objective from your JIST Card sounds good when you add it to the worksheet, you are done. If it doesn't, change it around a bit until it does. For example, if your JIST Card says you want a "Clerical/General Office" position, your phone script might say this:

"I am interested in a clerical or general office position."

Your Strengths

The Skills section of your JIST Card lists length of experience, training, education, special skills related to the job, and accomplishments. Use this information in your phone script.

Rewriting the content from this part of your JIST Card may take some time. The sentences in your phone script must sound natural when spoken. You may find it helpful to write and edit this section on a separate piece of paper before writing on the worksheet.

Read the final version out loud to hear how it sounds. Also read it to others, then make any final changes.

Your Good Worker Traits

Simply take the last sentence from your JIST Card and make these key traits into a sentence. For example, "Reliable, Hard Working, Learn Quickly" from a JIST Card might be written in a phone script as "I am reliable, hard working, and I learn quickly."

Your Goal

Your goal is to get an interview. The closing statement has been filled in for you because—that's right—it works! If you said, for example, "May I come in for an interview?" the employer could say no. And you don't want to make it easy for him to say no!

Your Telephone Contact Worksheet

Now it's time to complete your telephone contact worksheet.

Name: Hello, my name is _____

Objective: I am interested in a position as _____

_____

Strengths:_____

_____

_____

Good Worker Traits: _____

_____

_____

_____

The Goal: "When may I come in for an interview?"

The Final Script

After you have practiced your script several times, you may want to improve it. Write your final script here. Be sure to write it neatly and use complete sentences. Write the entire script, exactly as you will say it on the phone.

_____

_____

_____

_____

_____

_____

_____

_____

_____

_____

_____

_____

Tips for Effective Phone Contacts

Now that you have developed your phone script, you need to know how to use it effectively. Here are more tried and true tips:

Get to the Hiring Authority

You need to get directly to the person who would supervise you. Unless you want to work in the Personnel Department, you wouldn't normally ask to talk to someone who does.

Depending on the type and size of the organization you're calling, you should have a pretty good idea of the title of the person who would supervise you. In a small business you might ask to speak to the "person in charge." In a larger one, you would ask for the name of the person who is in charge of a particular department.

Get the Name of a Person

If you don't have the name of the person you need to speak to, ask for it. For example, ask for the name of the person in charge of the warehouse if that is where you want to work. Usually, you will be given the name and your call will be transferred to him immediately.

When you do get a name, get the correct spelling and write it down right away. Then you can use his name in your conversation.

Get Past the Secretary

In some cases, secretaries will try to screen out your call. If they find out you are looking for a job, they may transfer you to the Personnel Department or ask you to send an application or resume. Here are some things you can do:

Call back: Call back a day later and say you are getting ready to send some correspondence to the person who manages such and such. You want to use the correct name and title and request that they give you this information. This is true since you *will* be sending them something soon. And this approach usually gets you what you need. Say thank you and call back in a day or so. Then ask for the manager by name.

Call when the secretary is out: You are likely to get right through if you call when that secretary is out to lunch. Other good times are just before and after normal work hours. Less experienced staff members are likely to answer the phones and let you right through. The boss might also be in early or working late.

When Referred by Someone Else

It is always best to be referred by someone else. If this is the case, immediately give the name of the person who suggested you call. For example, say:

"Hello, Mr. Beetle. Joan Bugsby suggested I give you a call."

If the receptionist asks why you are calling, say:

"A friend of Mr. Beetle's suggested I give him a call about a personal matter."

When a friend of the employer recommends that you call, you usually get right through. It's that simple.

When Calling Someone You Know

Sometimes using your telephone script just as it is written on your worksheet will not make sense.

For example, if you are calling someone you know, you would normally begin with some friendly conversation before getting to the purpose of your call. Then, you could use your phone script by saying something like this:

"The reason I called is to let you know I am looking for a job, and I thought you might be able to help. Let me tell you a few things about myself. I am looking for a position as. . .(continue with the rest of your phone script here)"

There are many other situations where you will need to adapt your basic script. Use your own judgment on this. With practice, it becomes easier!

Get an Interview

The primary goal of a phone contact is to get an interview. To succeed, you must be ready to get past the first and even the second rejection.

Ask Three Times

You must practice asking three times for the interview! Here is an example:

1.   You: When may I come in for an interview?

       Employer: I don't have any positions open now.

2.   You: That's OK, I'd still like to come in to an interview to talk about future openings.

       Employer: I really don't plan on hiring within the next six months or so.

3.   You: Then I'd like to come in and learn more about what you do. I'm sure you know a lot about the industry, and I am looking for ideas on getting into it and moving up.

Although this approach does not always work, asking the third time works more often than most people would believe!

Arrange a Time

If the person agrees to an interview, arrange a specific time and date. If you are not sure of her name or address, call back later and ask the receptionist.

Sometimes an Interview Does Not Make Sense

Sometimes you will decide not to ask for an interview. The person may not seem helpful or you may have caught her at a busy time. If so, you take other approaches:

Get a referral: Ask for names of other people who might be able to help you. Find out how to contact them. Then add these new contacts to your job-search network!

Ask to call back: If your contact is busy when you call, ask if you can call back. Get a specific time and day to do this, and add the call to your to-do list for that day. If you do call back, she will be impressed. And she may give you an interview for just that reason.

Ask if it is OK to call back from time to time: Maybe she will hear of an opening or have some other information for you. Many job seekers get their best leads from a person they have checked back with several times!

Follow Up

With all your contacts, including phone calls, follow up. This effort can make a big difference. Here are the best ways to follow up:

Send a thank you note. It is good manners to thank the person who helped you. Send a thank you note right after the phone call. If you arranged for an interview, send a note saying you look forward to meeting her. If she gave you a referral to someone else, send her another note telling her how things turned out. Or send a thank you note telling her you followed up on her suggestion. Enclosing a JIST Card or resume is often a good idea, too.

Overcoming Fear, Part 2

Making phone calls is work. You are more likely to do it if you schedule your calls every day. It is easiest if you plan to make your calls at a certain time each day. You should also have a goal, so decide how many calls you will make per day. Most job seekers can make 10 to 20 calls per hour. And they often get an interview with this many calls. Not bad for an hour's work!

DOING WELL IN A JOB INTERVIEW

What Employers Really Want to Know

Interviewing for a job is one of the hardest parts of the job search. You may be a bit nervous about it yourself. You may have had a bad interview experience, and you don't look forward to another. Most people end up getting rejected. And they don't like it.

But it doesn't have to be that way. In your case, you know what you want to do. And you have the skills, experience, and training to do it. All you have to do is convince the employer that you can do the job. This chapter and Chapter Eleven show you how.

Employer Expectations

Employers use an interview to evaluate you. Will you be able to do the job? Will you be a good employee? If they don't believe you are qualified and willing to work hard, you won't get a job offer. If you do meet their expectations, you may get an offer—or a referral. So you need to know what to do and say in a job interview.

You looked at employer expectations in Chapter One. Because they are so important, let's review them here.

Expectation #1:   **Do You Look Like the Right Person?**
Appearance: First impressions do count!
- Personal appearance
- Manner
- Paper work

Expectation #2: **Can You Be Counted On?**
Dependability
- Can be trusted
- Gets things done on time
- Gets along well with others
- Is productive

Expectation #3: **Can You Do the Job?**
Skills, Experience, Training
- Experience
- Education and training
- Interests and hobbies
- Life experience
- Achievements
- Ability

In one way or another, interviewers must find out about all these things. At every point in the interview process, they are evaluating you—even when you might least expect it.

The following section breaks the interview into seven phases or sections. As you learn to handle each one, you will be better able to meet an employer's expectations. Then you will be much more likely to get a job offer!

Seven Phases of an Interview

No two interviews are alike. But there are similarities. If you look closely at the interview process, you can see separate phases. Looking at each phase will help you learn how to handle interviews well.

The phases are:

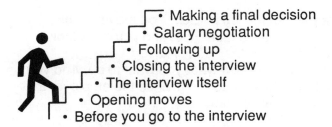

- Making a final decision
- Salary negotiation
- Following up
- Closing the interview
- The interview itself
- Opening moves
- Before you go to the interview

Every step of the interview is important. The following sections show you why and give you tips for handling each phase.

Phase 1: Before You Go to the Interview

Before you even meet, the interviewer can form an impression of you.

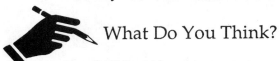 What Do You Think?

How? Write at least two ways:

1. _____

2. _____

There are many ways an interviewer can make judgments about you before you meet. For example, you may have spoken to the interviewer or her secretary on the phone. You may have sent her a resume or other correspondence. Or someone may have told her about you.

Before you meet an interviewer, here are some things to consider:

Appearance

You may not consider what follows as *appearance* issues, but they are. So be careful in all your early contacts with an employer. Do everything possible to create a good impression.

Dress and Grooming

How you dress and groom for an interview varies from job to job. You will have to make your own decisions about what is right for the job you're about to interview for.

Rule for interview dress and grooming:
Dress (and groom) like the interviewer is likely to be dressed—but cleaner.

You may not dress just like your supervisor, but looking like the boss is usually a good idea. Of course, different jobs and organizations require different styles of dress. For example, a person looking for a job as an auto mechanic would dress differently than one looking for an office job.

Because there are so many differences, there are no firm *rules* on how to dress. But there are things to avoid. Here are some important tips:

Don't wear jeans, tank tops, shorts, or other very casual clothes: Some clothing, even if it looks good on you, just isn't good for a serious interview. If you are in doubt about anything you're thinking of wearing, don't wear it.

Be conservative: An interview is not a good time to be trendy. Traditional styles are particularly important for office jobs and in large, formal organizations.

Check your shoes: One study found that employers reacted to the condition and style of a job seeker's shoes! Unshined shoes were an indication, they felt, of someone who would not work hard. Little things do count, so pay attention to everything you wear.

Colognes, aftershaves, make-up, jewelry: Again, be conservative. Keep your make-up simple and avoid too much of anything.

Careful grooming is a must: Get those hands and nails extra clean and manicured. Eliminate stray facial hairs. Get a simple hair style.

Spend some money if necessary: Get one well-fitting "interview outfit." Get your hair styled. Look a bit sharper than you usually do. If you have a limited budget, borrow something! It's that important.

Consider using a *uniform*: Some styles are almost always acceptable in certain jobs. For men working in an office, a conservative business suit, white shirt, and conservative tie are always acceptable. A less formal approach would include gray slacks, a blue blazer, white or blue shirt, and a conservative tie. For women, there are many more alternatives, but a simple tailored skirt, matching jacket, and white blouse are a safe choice. Women should not wear informal clothing to a job interview.

In jobs that don't require formal dress, plan to dress a few notches above the clothing you might normally wear in that job.

Discuss proper interview dress and grooming with friends and family before you finally decide for yourself. You can also get good books at the library covering helpful tips for "dressing for success." After you've thought about it, write here how you plan to dress and groom for an interview:

_____

_____

_____

_____

_____

Researching

Know as much as you can about the organization before you go to an important interview. Find out about the following things:

The Organization:
    Size, number of employees
    Major products or services
    Competitors and the competitive environment
    Major changes in policies or status
    Reputation, values
    Major weaknesses or opportunities

The Interviewer:
    Level and area of responsibility
    Special work-related projects, interests, and accomplishments
    Personal information (family, hobbies, etc.)
    What sort of boss he or she is
    Management style

The Position:
    Does an opening exist or do similar jobs exist?
    What happened to others in similar positions?
    Salary range and benefits
    Duties and responsibilities
    What the last person did wrong (so you can avoid it) or right (so you can emphasize it)

Get There Early

Get to the interview a few minutes early. Make sure you know how to get there, and allow plenty of time to get there. If necessary, call the receptionist for directions.

Final Grooming

Before you go in for the interview, stop in a rest room. Look at yourself in a mirror and make any final adjustments.

Waiting Room Behavior

Assume that interviewers will hear about everything you do in the waiting room. They will ask the receptionist how you conducted yourself—and how you treated the receptionist.

The Receptionist

The receptionist's opinion of you matters. So go out of your way to be polite and friendly. If you spoke to the receptionist on the phone, mention that and express appreciation for any help you were offered.

If the Interviewer is Late

If the interviewer is late, you are lucky. He will probably feel bad about keeping you waiting. And may give you better than average treatment to make up for it.

If you have to wait over 20 minutes or so, ask to reschedule your appointment at another time. You don't want to act as if you have nothing to do. And, again, the interviewer will probably make it up to you later.

Phase 2: Opening Moves

The first few minutes of an interview are very important. If you make a bad impression, you probably won't be able to change it.

The Impression You Make

You already know how important your dress and grooming are. What else do interviewers react to? List here at least three things interviewers can observe that would affect their impression of you.

1. _____
2. _____
3. _____

Interviewers react to many things you say and do during the first few minutes of an interview. Here are some of the things they mention most often:

Initial Greeting

Be ready for a friendly greeting! Show you are happy to be there. Although this is a business meeting, your social skills will be considered, too. A firm, but not crushing, handshake is needed unless the interviewer does not offer to shake hands.

Posture

How you stand and sit can make a difference. You look more interested if you lean forward in your chair when talking or listening. If you lean back, you may look *too* relaxed.

Voice

You may be nervous, but try to sound enthusiastic. Your voice should be neither too soft nor too loud. Practice sounding confident.

Eye Contact

People who don't look at a speaker's eyes are considered shy, insecure, and even dishonest. Although you should never stare, you look more confident when you look at the interviewer's eyes while you listen or speak.

Distracting Habits

You may have nervous habits you don't even notice. But pay attention! Most interviewers find such habits annoying. For example, do you:

Play with your hair or clothing?

Say something like "You know?" or "Uhh" over and over? You know what I mean?

The best way to see yourself as others do is to have someone videotape you while you role-play an interview. If that is not possible, become aware of how others see you and try to change negative behavior. Your friends and relatives can help you to notice any annoying habits you have that could bother an interviewer.

Establishing the Relationship

Almost all interviews begin with informal chitchat. Favorite subjects are the weather, whether you had any trouble getting there, and similar topics. This chatting seems to have nothing to do with the interview. But it does. These first few minutes allow an interviewer to relax you and find out how you relate to each other.

Write some things you could do to make a good impression during this time: _____

_____

_____

_____

There are many things you could do during the first few minutes of an interview. The following are some suggestions from experienced interviewers.

Allow things to happen: Relax. Don't feel you have to start a serious interview right away.

Smile: Look happy to be there and to meet the interviewer.

Use the interviewer's name: Be formal. Use "Mister Rogers" or "Ms. Evans" unless you are asked to use another name. Use their name as often as you can in your conversation.

Compliment something in the interviewer's office: Look for something you can compliment or something you have in common. Most offices have photographs or other things you can comment on. Say how great his kids look or ask whether she decorated the office herself.

Ask some opening questions: After a few minutes of friendly talk, you could ask a question to get things started. For example:

> "I'd like to know more about what your organization does. Would you mind telling me?"

or

> "I have a background in _____ and I'm interested in how these skills might be best used in an organization such as yours."

Phase 3: The Interview Itself

This is the most complicated part of the interview. And it can last from 15 to 45 minutes or more while the interviewer tries to find your strengths and weaknesses.

Interviewers may ask you almost anything. They are looking for any *problems* you may have. They also want to be convinced that you have the skills, experience, and personality to do a good job.

If you have made a good impression so far, you can use this phase to talk about your qualifications.

Answering Problem Questions

In one survey, employers said that over 90% of the people they interviewed for a job could not answer a problem question. Over 80% could not explain the skills they had for the job. This is a serious problem for most job seekers. It keeps many of them from getting a good job that will use their skills.

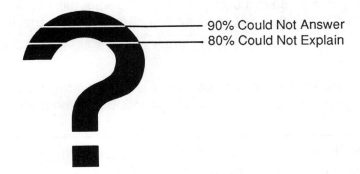

90% Could Not Answer
80% Could Not Explain

Ten Tough Questions

The following list shows the ten problem questions you are most likely to be asked during your interview. They may not be asked in just this way, but the interviewer *is* looking for answers to these questions.

Ten Most Frequently Asked Interview Questions

1. Why don't you tell me about yourself?
2. Why should I hire you?
3. What are your major strengths
4. What are your major weaknesses?
5. What sort of pay do you expect to receive?
6. How does your previous experience relate to the jobs we have here?
7. What are your plans for the future?
8. What will your former employers (or references) say about you?
9. Why are you looking for this sort of position and why here?
10. Why don't you tell me about your personal situation?

The next chapter shows you how to answer these questions. It also shows you how to answer other difficult questions. For now, let's look at the remaining phases of an interview.

Phase 4: Closing the Interview

All good things must end. You can close an interview as effectively as you began it.

Summarizing at the Finish

Take a few minutes to summarize the key points of the interview. If any problems or weaknesses came up, state why they will not keep you from doing a good job.

Point out the strengths you have for this job and why you believe you can do it well.

Ask for the Job

If you are interested in the job, say so! If you want this job, ask for it! Many employers hire one person over another just because one person really wants it. And says so.

The Call-Back Close

With the call-back close, you can end the interview to your advantage. It will take some practice. You may not be comfortable with it at first. But it works! Here's how:

The Call-Back Close

1. Thank the interviewer by name.
2. Express interest in the job and organization.
3. Arrange a reason and a time to call back.
4. Say good-bye.

Here's what you do:

Thank the interviewer by name: While shaking hands, say "Thank you (Mr. or Mrs. or Ms. Whomever) for your time today."

Express interest: Tell them you are interested in the position or organization (or both!), whichever makes sense. For example: "The position we discussed today is just what I have been looking for. And I am very impressed by your organization, too."

Arrange a reason and a time to call back: If the interviewer has been helpful, he won't mind your following up. It's important that you arrange a day and time to call. *Never* expect the employer to call you. Say something like this: "I'm sure I'll have questions. When would be the best time for me to get back to you."

Say good-bye: After you've set a time and date to call back, thank the interviewer by name and say good-bye. Like this, "Thank you, Mr. Pomeroy, for the time you gave me today. I will call you next Tuesday morning, between 9 and 10 o'clock."

Phase 5: Follow Up

You have left the interview and it's over. Right? Not really. You need to follow up! This can make the difference between your getting the job and someone else getting it. Here are some things you must do.

Send a thank you note: As soon as possible after the interview—no later than 24 hours—send a thank you note. Enclose a JIST Card, too.

Make notes: Write yourself notes about the interview while it is still fresh in your mind. You will not remember details in a week or so.

Follow up as promised: If you said you would call back next Tuesday at 9, do it. You will surely impress the interviewer with how organized you are.

Thank You Notes

Sending a thank you note is a simple act of appreciation that hardly anyone ever does. Thank you notes show your appreciation. And they also have practical benefits. People who receive them will remember you. But employers say they rarely get a thank you note. They describe people who do send them with positive terms, such as thoughtful, well-organized, and thorough.

A thank you note won't get you a job you're not qualified for, but it will impress people. When a job opens up, they will remember you. People in your job-search network will also be more interested in helping you. If they know of an opening or meet someone who does, they will think of you.

Here are some tips for preparing thank you notes:

Paper and envelope: Use a good quality note paper with matching envelope. Most stationery stores have them. Avoid cute covers. A simple "Thank You" on the front will do. Off-white and buff colors are good.

Typed vs. handwritten: Handwritten notes are fine unless your handwriting is illegible or sloppy. If so, type them.

Salutation: Unless you are thanking a friend or relative, don't use first names. Write "Dear Mrs. Krenshaw" rather than "Dear Vera." Include the date.

The note: Keep it short and friendly. This is not the place to write, "The reason you should hire me is. . . ." Remember, the note is a thank you for what the person did. It is not a hard-sell pitch for what you want. As appropriate, be specific about when you will next be in contact. If you plan to meet with the person soon, still send a note saying you looking forward to meeting them and name the date and time.

Your signature: Use your first and last names. Avoid initials and make your signature legible.

When to send it: Send your note no later than 24 hours after you make contact. Ideally, you should write it immediately after the contact while the details are fresh in your mind. Always send a note after an interview, even if things did not go well.

Enclosure: Depending on the situation, a JIST Card is often the ideal enclosure. It's a *soft sell* and provides your phone number if the person should wish to reach you. ("Gosh, that job just opened up! Who was that person who called me last week?") Make sure your note cards are at least as big as the JIST Card so you don't have to fold it.

2234 Riverwood Ave.
Philadelphia, PA 17963
April 16, 1992

Ms. Helen A. Colcord
Henderson & Associates, Inc.
1801 Washington Blvd., Suite 1201
Philadelphia, PA 17963

Dear Ms. Colcord:

Thank you for sharing your time with me so generously today. I really appreciated seeing your state-of-the-art computer equipment.

Your advice has already proved helpful. I have an appointment to meet with Mr. Robert Hopper on Friday. As you anticipated, he does intend to add more computer operators in the next few months.

In case you think of someone else who might need a person like me, I'm enclosing another JIST Card. I will let you know how the interview with Mr. Hopper goes.

Sincerely,

William Richardson

William Richardson

Kay Howell
Apartment 3C
1030 College Avenue
Denver, Colorado 80260

October 22, 1992

Mr. Robert A. Hernandez
Manager, Data Processing Division
Harmon Enterprises
4648 Pearl Street
Denver, Colorado 80442

Dear Mr. Hernandez:

Thank you for meeting with me today. I'm impressed by the high standards your department maintains — the more I heard and saw the more interested I became in working for your firm.

As we agreed, I will call you next Monday, October 28. In the meantime, I would be pleased to answer any additional questions you may have.

Sincerely,
Kay Howell

Phase 6: Negotiating Salary and Benefits

Let's imagine that the job you are interviewing for sounds ideal for you. But you still have to answer some tough questions.

What Would You Say?

Suppose the interviewer asks you "What do you expect to get paid for this position?" What would you say? Write it here:

_____

_____

_____

_____

_____

Whatever you say, you will probably lose. Suppose the employer was willing to pay $15,000 per year (or $7.00 per hour or whatever). If you say you will take $13,500, guess what you will be paid. That may have been the most expensive ten seconds in your life!

There are other ways you can lose, too. The employer may decide not to hire you at all. He or she may think they need a person who is worth $15,000—which leaves you out. If you were clever, you may have asked for $16,500 and hoped you would get it. You could lose here, too. Many employers would assume you'll be unhappy with the salary they had in mind. Even if you would have been happy to have it.

Salary Negotiation Rule 1: Never discuss salary until you are being offered the job.

And now you understand why.

You will learn more rules about negotiating salaries in the next chapter. This is one of the problem questions most job seekers have trouble answering.

Phase 7: Making a Final Decision

The interview process is not completely over until you accept a job. This can sometimes be an easy decision to make. There are other times when deciding can be very hard.

The following form shows you how to put the positives and negatives of a difficult decision down on paper. People who use this process tend to make better decisions. Some research shows they also tend to be happier with what they did, even when it did not work out. You can use this form to help you make any decision.

This example shows how one person used the form to consider a job offer. The final decision will always be yours to make, but this form can help you make a good decision.

Decision-Making Worksheet

Option Considered: _Director of Sales, Farkel's Foods_

	Positives	Negatives
Tangible Things for *Me*	1. More money 2. Work I will like better. 3. An office of my own. 4. A chance to travel.	1. Lots of pressure & long hours. 2. Less job security. 3. My boss is known to have a bad temper.
Tangible Things for *Others*	1. Can move back to the country 2. Can afford better clothes + more recreation for the family 3. Can start a college fund for the kids.	1. I'll be away from home more often. 2. Less private time. 3. More driving. 4. Will be taking work home more often.
Self Approval / Disapproval	1. I get to set my own goals & time tables, at least to a point. 2. I'll have a chance to become better known in the field.	1. I may feel guilty about being on the road so much and away from the family. 2. Other people in the firm may resent my status
Social Approval / Disapproval	1. My friends & family will be impressed. 2. Professionally, this company is a leader.	1. I'll have to prove myself to some of our old time sales reps. + customers.

You have now learned about the seven phases of an interview. In the next chapter you will learn to answer problem interview questions. Knowing how to answer these questions will help you to get the job you want!

ANSWERING PROBLEM QUESTIONS

Don't Be Caught by Surprise

In Chapter Ten, you learned that an interview has seven phases. The third phase is the interview itself. This is the most complicated part of the interview. And it can last from 15 to 45 minutes or more. This is when the interviewer tries to find out about your your strengths and weaknesses.

Interviewers may ask you almost anything. They are looking for any problems you may have. They also want to be convinced that you have the skills, experience, and personality to do a good job.

Answering Problem Questions

The biggest challenge most job seekers face in this phase of an interview is answering a problem question. For example, write an answer to the following question. Keep your interview response short and positive.

"What are your plans for the future?"

_____

_____

_____

Are you satisfied with what you wrote? Would your answer make a good impression on an interviewer? Would your answer meet one or more of an employer's expectations?

If you are like most job seekers, you can learn to do better. In one survey, employers said that over 90% of the people they interviewed could not answer a problem question. Over 80% could not describe the skills they had for the job. This is a serious problem for most job seekers. It keeps many of them from getting a good job that will use their skills.

The following list shows the ten questions you are most likely to be asked during your interview. This is the same list you saw in Chapter 10. The question may not be asked in these exact words, but the interviewer is looking for answers to these questions.

Ten Most Frequently Asked Interview Questions

1. Why don't you tell me about yourself?
2. Why should I hire you?
3. What are your major strengths?
4. What are your major weaknesses?
5. What sort of pay do you expect to receive?
6. How does your previous experience relate to the jobs we have here?
7. What are your plans for the future?
8. What will your former employers (or references) say about you?
9. Why are you looking for this sort of position and why here?
10. Why don't you tell me about your personal situation?

Besides these questions, there are hundreds of others you could be asked. You could learn to answer some of them here, but the interviewer may ask you different ones. So it is more important to learn a method for answering *any* question than to memorize answers to some. Take some time now to learn a method for all kinds of difficult questions.

Answering the Toughest Questions

Look at the following "Three Steps To Answering Problem Questions." This gives you a simple way of looking at each question you are asked in an interview. With practice, you can use the steps to answer any interview question.

Three Steps to Answering Problem Questions

Understand What Is Really Being Asked!
The question usually relates to Employer Expectation #2 about your adaptive skills and personality:
- Can we depend on you?
- Are you easy to get along with?
- Are you a good worker?

The question may also relate to Employer Expectation #3:
- Do you have the experience and training to do the job if we hire you?

STEP 2

Answer the Question Briefly.
- Acknowledge the facts.
- But present them as advantages, not disadvantages.

STEP 3

Answer the Real Concern by Presenting Your Skills!
- Base your answer on your key skills, as listed on your JIST Card.
- Give examples to support your skills statements.

Notice how important it is to know what an employer expects. If you don't remember, look at Chapter One. The three major employer's expectations are listed there.

Using Three Steps to Answer a Problem Question

Let me give you an example. Here is one of the ten questions you are likely to be asked in an interview:

"What are your plans for the future?"

How would you answer this? Let's use the three steps to see how you could give an honest answer that meets the employer's expectations.

Step 1: Understand What Is Really Being Asked

What does the interviewer really want to know? Look at the box with Three Steps to Answering Problem Questions, and decide what the employer is looking for with this question. Write what you think is really being asked.

_____

_____

_____

_____

_____

In this case, the interviewer probably wants to know if you are going to remain on the job long enough. And he probably wants to know that you *want* this particular kind of job in his type of organization. Saying that you hope to sail around the world may be interesting, but it would not be a good response.

Step 2: Answer the Question Briefly

First, answer the actual question as it is asked. For example, you could say:

"There are many things I want to do over the next five years. One is to get settled into the career I have decided on and learn as much as I can."

This is a brief answer to the question. It doesn't say much, but it allows you to begin answering the real question. And the real question is probably a form of Employer's Expectation #2, "Can I depend on you?"

Step 3: Answer the Real Concern by Presenting Your Related Skills
Here is a sample response:

"I've had a number of jobs (or one, been unemployed, or other experiences. . .) and I have learned to value a good, stable position. My variety of experiences is an asset because I have learned so many things I can now apply to this position. I am looking for a position where I can get totally involved, work hard, and do well."

Depending on your own situation, there are many other things you could say. This response emphasizes the job seeker's stability. But, as brief as it is, this answer meets the employer's expectations.

Review your earlier answer to this question. If you are like most job seekers, your response could be improved. Using the three steps to answering a problem question, rewrite your answer.

Ten Most Frequently Asked Questions

Now, let's look at some tips for answering the top ten interview questions. Your own responses will be different from the examples given here. But if you use the three steps to answering problem questions, you can learn how to answer each of these questions effectively. Then you'll be ready to do better than 90% of the job seekers you are competing with.

Question 1: Why don't you tell me about yourself?

The interviewer does not want to know your life history! Instead, he or she wants you to tell how your background relates to doing the job. Here is a sample response:

"I grew up in the Southwest and my parents and one sister still live there. I always did well in school, and by the time I graduated from high school, knew I wanted to work in a business setting. I had taken typing and other business classes and had done well in them. And the jobs I've had while going to school have taught me how many small businesses are run. In one of these jobs, I was given complete responsibility for the night operations of a wholesale grocery business that grossed over two million dollars a year. I learned there how to supervise others and solve problems under pressure."

This answer gives a very brief personal history and then gets right into the skills and experiences this job seeker has. A different job would require you to stress different skills. Your personal history is different, but you can still follow the three basic steps to answering a problem question.

How would you answer this question in an interview? Write your own answer to the question: ____

_____

_____

_____

_____

_____

Question 2: Why should I hire you?

This is the most important question of all! If you don't have a good reason, why *should* anyone hire you? It is not often asked this clearly, but this is *the* question behind many interview questions.

The best answer is to show how you can solve a problem for them, help the business make more money, or provide something else of value that they need. Think about the most valuable thing you can do for an organization. That is probably what you should include in your answer.

Here is an example from a person with recent training but little work experience:

"I have over two years of training in this field and know about all the latest equipment and methods. That means I can get right to work and be productive almost right away. I am also willing to work hard to learn new things. During the entire time I went to school, I worked a full-time job to help earn the tuition. I learned to work hard and concentrate on what was important. I expect to do the same thing here. Since I won't be going to school now, I plan on putting in extra time after regular work hours to learn anything this job needs."

Now think about the job you want. What strengths can you bring to that job? Then answer the question:

_____

_____

_____

_____

_____

_____

_____

_____

Question 3: What are your major strengths?

This is a direct question with little hidden meaning. Answer it by emphasizing the adaptive skills you defined in Chapter Three. These are the skills employers are most concerned about (Employer Expectations #2). Here is one answer from a person who had little prior work experience:

> "I think one of them is that you can depend on me. I work very hard to meet deadlines and don't need a lot of supervision in doing it. If I don't know what to do, I don't mind asking either. In high school I got a solid B-plus average even though I was very involved in sports. I always got my assignments in on time and somehow found the time to do extra credit work, too."

Review Chapter Three and use at least two of your top adaptive skills in answering this question:

_____

_____

_____

_____

_____

Question 4: What are your major weaknesses?

This is a question most job seekers don't handle well. If you tell what you do poorly, you may not get the job. If you say you have no weaknesses, the interviewer won't believe you. Ask yourself what the interviewer really wants to know. She wants to know that you are aware of your weaknesses. And that you have learned to overcome them so that they don't affect your work.

Using the three-step process, the second step would result in a response like this:

> "I do have some weaknesses. For example, in previous jobs I would get annoyed with co-workers who didn't work as hard as I did. I sometimes said so to them and several times refused to do their work when they asked me to."

But the response should not end there. The third step would result in a statement like this:

> "But I have learned to deal with this better. I still work hard, but I let the supervisor deal with another worker's problems. And I've also gained some skills as a supervisor myself. I've learned to motivate others to do more because they want to, not because I want them to."

Did you notice that this weakness isn't such a weakness at all? Many of our strengths began in failure. We learned from them and got better.

List some weaknesses of this type that you could use in your own answer.

_____

_____

_____

Now, pick one of these and use it to answer the question. Use the three steps!

_____

_____

_____

_____

Question 5: What sort of pay do you expect to receive?

Knowing how to answer this question could be worth a lot of money to you! In Chapter 10 you learned that one of the interview phases is negotiating salary. This question deals with the the same issue. In that chapter, you learned this important rule in salary negotiation:

Salary Negotiation Rule 1: Never discuss salary until you are being offered the job.

It might be helpful to review why this is so before you continue. Here are a few paragraphs from that chapter to refresh your memory:

Whatever you say, you will probably lose. Suppose the employer was willing to pay $15,000 per year (or $7.00 per hour or whatever). If you say you will take $13,500, guess what you will be paid. That may have been the most expensive ten seconds in your life!

There are other ways you can lose, too. The employer may decide not to hire you at all. He or she may think they really need a person who is worth $15,000—which leaves you out. If you were clever, you may have asked for $16,500 and hoped you would get it. You could lose here, too. Many employers would assume you'll be unhappy with the salary they had in mind. Even if you would have been happy to have it.

Good advice. But you didn't really learn how to answer the salary question. For this question, you need to remember the following three rules:

Salary Negotiation Rule 2: Know the probable salary range.

Before the interview, you need to know what similar jobs in similar types of organizations pay. This will give you an idea of what the position is likely to pay. To find out, ask others in similar jobs. The library is a good source of salary information. Ask the research librarian. You can also call your local state Employment Service's statistical office. They are required to keep this information for each area.

Salary Negotiation Rule 3: Bracket your salary range.

If you think the employer pays between $14,000 and $16,000/year, state your own range as "mid to upper teens." That covers the amount the employer probably had in mind and gives you room to get more. You have *bracketed* the amount you are willing to accept to include their probable range and a bit more. Here is how it would look.

If They Pay:	You Say:
$5/hour	5 to 7 dollars per hour
$13,000/year	low to mid teens
$16,500/year	mid to upper teens
$18,500/year	upper teens to low twenties
$27,500/year	upper twenties to low thirties

Salary Negotiation Rule 4: Never say no to a job offer before it is made or until 24 hours have passed.

Remember, the objective of an interview is to get a job offer. Many job seekers get screened out early in the interview by discussing salary. If you give the impression that the job doesn't pay what you had hoped, or if it pays more, you could get screened out. The best approach is to avoid discussing salary until you are being offered the job. If the money is not what you had in mind, say you want to consider the offer and will call back the next day. You can always turn it down then.

You may also say that if the salary were higher you would take the position. Perhaps you could be given more responsibility to justify a higher wage? Or you could negotiate an increase after a certain period of time.

Do not negotiate like this unless you are willing to give up the offer. But you just might be able to get a counter offer that you would accept.

Question 6: How does your previous experience relate to the jobs we have here?

This one requires a direct response. This question is saying, "Can you prove you have the experience and skills to do the job?" It is directly related to Employer's Expectation #3. In some cases, other people with better credentials than yours will want the job you're after. You should mention this, then explain why you are a better choice.

Here is an example of how one person handled this situation:

"As you know, I have over five years of experience in a variety of jobs. While this job is in a different industry, it requires my same skills in managing people and meeting the public. In fact, my daily contact with large numbers of people on previous jobs has taught me how to handle things under pressure. I feel very able to deal with pressure and to get the job done."

One of the jobs this person had was as a waitress. She had to learn to handle people under pressure in such a job. By presenting the *skills* she used, her answer tells us she could use the same skills in other jobs.

Be sure to mention any specific skills or training you have that will help you do the job. Include your greatest job-related strengths in your own answer to this question:

_____

_____

_____

_____

_____

Question 7: What are your plans for the future?

As you recall, we covered this question earlier in this chapter. This question is really asking whether you are likely to remain on the job. But an employer has many concerns, depending on your situation.

This question also asks:

- Will you be happy with the salary? (If not, you may leave.)
- Will you leave to raise a family or relocate because of your spouse's job transfer?
- Do you have a history of leaving jobs after a short stay? (If so, it seems likely you will do this again.)
- Are you overqualified (and likely to be unhappy in this job)?

There may be other concerns, too. You may wish to practice answering this question again. If so, try to put yourself in an employer's place. Then answer the real question. Try to bring up anything in your own life situation that some employers might be concerned about.

_____

_____

_____

_____

_____

Question 8: What will your former employers (teachers, or other references) say about you?

This question again goes after Employer's Expectation #2. The interviewer really wants to know about your adaptive skills and whether you can be depended on. Are you easy to get along with? Are you reliable?

Many employers will check your references. So if you are less than honest about problems in previous jobs, you could get caught! If everyone you ever worked for thinks you are great, answering this question will be easy. But almost everyone has had some type of a problem. If the interviewer is likely to find out about your problem by checking with previous employers, honesty could be the best policy. Tell it like it was and accept responsibility for being part of the problem.

Many interviewers have been fired sometime in their careers. It's no sin and often has little to do with being a good worker. If you learned something from the experience, say so.

In a way, this question is similar to asking you for your major weakness. The right answer to this question can get you the job— even if you have to reveal some negative information. Here is an example:

"If you check with my two previous employers, they will both tell you that I am a good worker and that I do things right. But you may find out that one of them is not too enthusiastic about me. I really can't explain why we did not get along. I tried to do my best, but she passed me over for merit raises twice.

She will tell you that I got the work done, but she may also tell you that I was not willing to socialize with the other workers after hours. I had a new baby and I was working full time. I was very reliable, but it was true that I didn't go out two or three times a week with the others. I left on my own and got my next job with a boss who will say wonderful things about me. But I thought you might want to know."

If you do expect a problem from a previous employer, try to find out exactly what he or she will say. If possible, talk it over so you know exactly what they will say when giving a reference. Ask them to write you a letter of reference. Usually they will not be too negative in a letter and your new employer may accept the letter and not call.

If you still know that this employer will give you a negative reference, think of someone else you worked with closely in the same organization. Ask that person to give you a reference instead.

Write your own response to this question:

_____

_____

_____

_____

_____

Question 9: Why are you looking for this sort of position and why here?

Employers know that you will do better in the job you really want. Employers want to make sure you know what you want. They also want you to tell them what you like about the job. And what you like about doing this job in their organization. The closer you come to wanting what they have, the better.

The best answer for this is the absolute truth. You need a clear idea of the type of job you want. You also need to know the type of organization and people you want to work with. You gathered all of this information earlier in this book. And if you are interviewing for a job you want, in a place where you think you would enjoy working, answering this question should be easy.

Take another look at your reasons for wanting this type of job. Select your top two reasons. Be sure to include these in your answer. Since you don't yet have a particular employer to respond to, use your imagination to decide what the company you're interviewing with is like. Then tell them what you like about their organization.

_____

_____

_____

_____

_____

Question 10: Why don't you tell me about your personal situation?

Very few interviewers will ask this question so directly. But they *do* want to know. They will try to find out in casual conversation. While you may feel that this is none of their business, they probably won't hire you unless they feel comfortable about your response.

If you follow the three-step process, you would first ask yourself what are they really asking? It is clear enough that they are concerned about Employer's Expectation #2. The issue is whether you can be counted on. They will look for signs that you are unstable or unreliable.

The question behind the question asked is usually one of these:

The Question	An Employer's Real Concern
Are you single?	Will you stay?
Are you married?	Will you devote the necessary time?
Do you have marital or family troubles?	Missed work, poor performance, poor interpersonal skills?
Do you handle money and personal responsibilities poorly?	Theft of property? Irresponsible job-related decisions?
Do you live in a good, stable home?	Socio-economic bias, renters less stable than owners.
How do you use your leisure time?	Drinking, socially unacceptable behavior?
Do you have young children?	Days off and child-care problems?

You could argue that interviewers would be unfair and biased if they asked some of these questions. But you must understand that they really only need to be told that you can be counted on. Even if you just moved here, even if you have kids, even if you are single.

Here are some sample responses to these questions. If one or more of these life situations are true for you, and they do not limit your ability to work, tell the interviewer. Even if he or she doesn't ask.

When responding to a question about your personal life, be friendly and positive. The message to give is that your personal situation will not hurt your ability to do a good job. Indeed, your situation could offer some benefits to the company.

Young children at home: "I have two children, both in school. Child care is no problem since they stay with a good friend."

Single head of household: "I'm not married and have two children at home. It is very, very important to me to have a steady income, and so child care is no problem."

Young and single: "I'm not married, and if I should marry, that would not change my plans for a full-time career. For now, I can devote my full attention to my career.

Just moved here: "I've decided to settle here in Depression Gulch permanently. I've rented an apartment, and the six moving vans are unloading there now."

Relatives, childhood: "I had a good childhood. Both of my parents still live within an hour's flight from here, and I see them several times a year."

Leisure: "For relaxation I grow worms in my spare time and am a member of the American Worm Growers Association."

Or you may prefer, "My time is family-centered when I'm not working. I'm also active in several community organizations and spend at least some time each week in church activities."

All these responses could be expanded, but they should give you an idea of approaches you can take.

Other "Problem" Questions

Most people feel that employers will hold one particular thing against them. It may be something obvious, like age (being "too old" or "too young"). Or something not so obvious, like not having a degree. Or whatever. And most employers do hold one or another unfair bias.

But employers are also people. They generally try to be fair. And as employers, they are very interested in getting a good worker.

Your job is to make it easy for an interviewer to find out you *can* do the job. The problem is that many interviewers may *assume* you have a problem. They may not ask you directly if their assumption is true for you. And you won't have a chance to tell them that, in your case, the "rule" is not true.

For example, if you are more than a little overweight, some employers may feel you will be sick a lot or be slow in your work. The interviewer will probably not bring it up. But he or she may not hire you either. Unless, somehow, you convince him that you are healthy, reliable, and quick.

You can bring up your weight or not. It is up to you. But it would be wise, if you do not bring it up directly, to emphasize that you do not fit any stereotype.

In almost all cases, the employer's assumptions have to do with, once again, Employer's Expectation 2. They need to know that they can depend on you to do the job. And if they don't ask and you don't tell them, who will?

Here are sample statements covering typical "problems" employers may be concerned about. Some are not fair or accurate assumptions. As a job seeker, though, you need to deal with what is real. Once you have the job, you can show them what is true for you.

Too old: "I am a very stable worker requiring very little training. I have been dependable all my life, and I am at a point in my career where I don't plan on changing jobs. I still have ten years of working until I plan on retiring, which is probably longer than the average young person stays in a position these days."

Too young: "I don't have any bad work habits to break, so I can be quickly trained to do things the way you want. I plan on working hard to get established. I'll also work for less money than a more experienced worker."

Prison (or arrest) record: "You need to know that I've spent time in jail. I learned my lesson and paid my debt to society for a mistake I have not repeated. While there, I studied hard and earned a certificate in this trade. I was in the top one-third of my class."

Physical limitations: "Thank you for the job offer. Before I accept, you should know that I have a minor physical limitation, but it will not affect my performance on the job. . . ."

Unemployed: "I've been between jobs now for three months. During that time, I've carefully researched what I want to do and now I'm certain. Let me explain. . . ."

Overweight: "You may have noticed that I am a tad overweight. Some people think that overweight people are slow, won't work hard, or will be absent frequently. But let me tell you about myself. . . ."

Gender: "Not many women (or men) are interested in these kinds of positions, so let me tell you why I am. . . ."

Race: The best approach here is to assume there is no problem with your race. There often is not and if there is, there shouldn't be. Present your skills, rest your case, send a thank you note, and go on to set up the next interview. This advice is the same for all job-seekers!

Physical disability: Don't be defensive or clinical. If your disability is obvious, you bring it up in a matter of fact way. People will want to know that your disability will not be a problem, so explain why it won't be. Then emphasize why you can do the job better than the next job-seeker.

Illegal Questions

Some people argue that some of the questions in the previous section are illegal to ask. Some of the questions, if they were asked as presented, *would* be in poor taste. But this is a free country. Anyone can ask anything they want. It is what an interviewer *does* with the information that can be a problem. Hiring or not hiring people based on certain criteria is illegal.

As a job seeker, what's more important is whether or not you want the job. You don't have to answer any question if you don't want to. But you should understand by now that the question was probably intended to find out if you will be a good employee. If you want the job, tell them that you do. If you don't like the interviewer or the way he or she asked the question, you can always say so.

Fortunately, most employers are just like you are. They will be sensitive to your feelings and will treat you as an adult. It is your responsibility to convince them you will be a good employee. Do not leave their impressions to chance. Tell them why they should hire you!

50 More Questions

Here is a list of 50 interview questions. It came from a survey of 92 companies who conduct student interviews. Look for questions you would have trouble answering. These are the ones you need answers to!

Common Interview Questions

1. In what school activities have you participated? Why? Which do you enjoy the most?
2. How do you spend your spare time? What are your hobbies?
3. Why do you think you might like to work for our company?
4. What jobs have you held? How were they obtained, and why did you leave?
5. What courses did you like best? Least? Why?
6. Why did you choose your particular field of work?
7. What percentage of your school expense did you earn? How?
8. What do you know about our company?
9. Do you feel that you have received good general training?
10. What qualifications do you have that make you feel that you will be successful in your field?
11. What are your ideas on salary?
12. If you were starting school all over again, what courses would you take?
13. Can you forget your education and start from scratch?
14. How much money do you hope to earn at age 25? 30? 40?
15. Why did you decide to go to the school you attended?
16. What was your rank in your graduating class in high school? Other schools?
17. Do you think that your extracurricular activities were worth the time you devoted to them? Why?
18. What personal characteristics are necessary for success in your chosen field?
19. Why do you think you would like this particular type of job?
20. Are you looking for a permanent or temporary job?
21. Are you primarily interest in making money or do you feel that service to your fellow human beings is a satisfactory accomplishment?
22. Do you prefer working with others or by yourself?
23. Can you take instructions without feeling upset?
24. Tell me a story!
25. What have you learned from some of the jobs you have held?
26. Can you get recommendations from previous employers?
27. What interests you about our product or service?
28. What was your record in the military service?
29. What do you know about opportunities in the field in which you are trained?
30. How long do you expect to work?
31. Have you ever had any difficulty getting along with fellow students and faculty? Fellow workers?
32. Which of your school years was most difficult?
33. Do you like routine work?
34. Do you like regular work?
35. What is your major weakness?
36. Define cooperation.
37. Will you fight to get ahead?
38. Do you have an analytical mind?
39. Are you willing to go where the company sends you?
40. What job in our company would you choose if you were entirely free to do so?
41. Have you plans for further education?
42. What jobs have you enjoyed the most? The least? Why?
43. What are your own special abilities?
44. What job in our company do you want to work toward?
45. Would you prefer a large or a small company? Why?
46. How do you feel about overtime work?
47. What kind of work interests you?
48. Do you think that grades should be considered by employers?
49. Are you interested in research?
50. What have you done that shows initiative and willingness to work?

Plus One More

What is the one question you are most afraid an employer will ask? Write it here. Then use the three-step process to give a positive answer that an employer could accept.

The question:_____

_____

The answer:_____

_____

_____

_____

_____

_____

_____

_____

There you have it. You are now better prepared for a job interview than most other job seekers. If you do well, you will be considered for jobs over people with better credentials. The more interviews you have, the better you will get. And you will get job offers.

YOUR RESUME

The Write Way to Success

This chapter gives you a brief introduction to resumes and cover letters. Samples of each are provided as well as tips for writing and using them effectively.

You Need a Resume Because. . .

Some experts now say that resumes are not necessary. Their point is that you should base your job search on personal contacts, not paper. I agree. But there are two good reasons that you *should* have a resume.

Why you need a resume:

1. Employers expect you to have them.
2. A good resume will help you decide what you have to offer an employer.

Employers use resumes to find out about your credentials and experience. Covering these details in an interview is not the best use of that valuable time. A well-written resume also forces you to summarize the highlights of your experience. When you've done this, you are better able to talk about yourself during the interview.

Tips for Using a Resume

At best, a resume will help you get an interview. However, there are better ways of getting one—as you've learned in earlier chapters of this book. Yet many books continue to tell job seekers to send out lots of resumes in hopes of getting an interview. Here is better advice. Use your resume in the following ways.

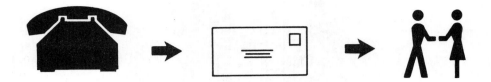

- Get the interview first. It is almost always better to contact the employer by phone or direct contact. Send your resume *after* you schedule an interview so the employer can read about you before your meeting. Valuable interview time will be spent discussing your skills, not your education.
- Send your resume or JIST Card to an interviewer after an information interview.
- Send copies of your resume and JIST Card to everyone in your growing job-search network. They can pass them along to others who might be interested.
- If you can't make direct contact, send your resume in the traditional way. An example would be answering a want ad with only a box number for an address. But don't expect much to happen.

Resume Basics

Here are some rules to follow when making your resume.

Write it yourself: Look at examples of resumes, but don't copy them. Your resume won't sound like you and many employers will know you didn't write it yourself.

Make every word count: Limit your resume to one page—two at the most. After you have a first draft, edit it at least two more times. If a word or phrase does not support your ability to do the job, cut it out.

Make it error free: Ask someone else to look for grammar and spelling errors. Check each word again before you have it printed and send it to an employer. It is amazing how many errors can get into the final version.

Make it look good: Have it typed professionally and copied on a good quality paper. Appearance, as you know, makes a lasting impression.

Stress your accomplishments: A resume is no place to be humble.

Be specific: Give facts and numbers. Instead of saying you are good with people, say "I supervised and trained three people in the mail room and increased their productivity by 30%." Now that means something!

Don't delay: Many job seekers say they are still improving their resume when they should be out looking for a job. A better approach is to do a simple, error-free resume at first. Then actively look for a job. You can always work on a better version at night and on weekends.

Keep it lively: Use action verbs and short sentences. Avoid negatives of any kind. Emphasize accomplishments and results.

Two Types of Resumes

Resume styles vary. The two most common types are *chronological* and *skills* resumes. Each has its advantages. This chapter shows you how to develop both of these types and shows you samples of each. There are also samples of a third type, the *combination* resume. This resume combines parts of both the chronological and the skills resumes. Examples of it are also provided.

The Chronological Resume

Chronology refers to time. A *chronological* resume begins with your most recent experiences and moves back in time. This type of resume has been used for many years. It is fine if you have a good work history and want your next job to be similar to the last one.

Look at the sample Chronological Resume. Notice the job objective and how the job seeker's experience is organized.

While this resume could be improved, it does present the facts and would be an acceptable resume for many employers. The Improved Chronological Resume is for the same person but additional content and other improvements have been added.

Because it is easy to create, I suggest that you write a simple chronological resume before making a *better* one. Then you can get started on your job search immediately. You might even get a job offer before you finish your improved version!

Judith J. Jones
115 South Hawthorne Avenue
Chicago, Illinois 46204

(317) 653-9217 (home)
(317) 272-7608 (leave message)

JOB OBJECTIVE

Desire a position in the office management, secretarial or clerical area. Prefer a position requiring responsibility and a variety of tasks.

EDUCATION AND TRAINING

Acme Business College, Indianapolis, Indiana — graduate of a one year business - secretarial program, 1982.

John Adams High School, South Bend, Indiana — Diploma, business education.

U.S. Army — Financial procedures, accounting functions.

Other: Continuing Education classes and workshops in Business communication, scheduling systems, and customer relations.

EXPERIENCE

1981 to 1982 — Returned to school to complete and update my business skills. Learned word processing and other new office techniques.

1979 to 1981 — Claims Processor, Blue Spear Insurance Co., Indianapolis, Indiana. Handled customer medical claims, used a CRT, filed, miscellaneous clerical duties.

1978 to 1979 — Sales Clerk, Judy's Boutique, Indianapolis, Indiana. Responsible for counter sales, display design, and related tasks.

1977 to 1979 — E4, U.S. Army. Assigned to various stations as a specialist in finance operations. Promoted prior to honorable discharge.

Previous jobs — Held part-time and summer jobs throughout High School.

PERSONAL

I am reliable, hard working, and good with people.

Judith J. Jones
115 South Hawthorne Avenue
Chicago, Illinois 46204

(317) 653-9217 (home)
(317) 272-7608 (message)

POSITION DESIRED

Seeking position requiring excellent management and secretarial skills in office environment. Position could require a variety of tasks including typing, word processing, accounting/bookkeeping functions, and customer contact.

EDUCATION AND TRAINING

Acme Business College, Indianapolis, Indiana. Completed one year program in Professional Secretarial and Office Management. Grades in top 30% of my class. Courses: word processing, accounting theory and systems, time management, basic supervision & others.

John Adams High School, South Bend, Indiana. Graduated with emphasis on business and secretarial courses. Won shorthand award.

Other: Continuing education at my own expense (Business Communications, Customer Relations, Computer Applications, other courses).

EXPERIENCE

1981 to 1982 — Returned to Business School to update skills. Advanced coursework in accounting and office management. Learned to operate word processing equipment including Wang, IBM, DEC. Gained operating knowledge of computers.

1979 to 1981 — Claims Processor, Blue Spear Insurance Company, Indianapolis, Indiana. Handled 50 complex medical insurance claims per day — 18% above departmental average. Received two merit raises for performance.

1978 to 1979 — Assistant Manager, Judy's Boutique, Indianapolis. Managed sales, financial records, inventory, purchasing, correspondence & related tasks during owner's absence. Supervised four employees. Sales increased 15% during my tenure.

1976 to 1978 — Finance Specialist (E4), U.S. Army. Responsible for the systematic processing of 500 invoices per day from commercial vendors. Trained and supervised eight others. Devised internal system allowing 15% increase in invoices processed with a decrease in personnel.

1972 to 1976 — Various part time and summer jobs through high school. Learned to deal with customers, meet deadlines and other skills.

SPECIAL SKILLS AND ABILITIES

80 words per minute on electric typewriter, more on word processor; can operate most office equipment. Good math skills. Accept supervision, able to supervise others. Excellent attendance record.

PERSONAL

I have excellent references, learn quickly, and am willing to relocate.

Some Tips on Writing a Superior Resume

There are many things you can do to make your resume stand out. You can use the following tips in all types of resumes.

Your name: Use your formal name instead of a nickname.

Address: Avoid abbreviations and include your zip code. If you might move, use a relative's address or arrange with the post office to forward your mail to your new address.

Telephone number: Include your area code. If your home phone is not always answered during the day, give a second number. It's important for employers to be able to reach you, even if they can only leave messages.

Job objective: Include your job objective in all but the most basic resume. Look at the examples to see how others have handled this. Notice that Judith didn't narrow down her options by saying "secretary" (a job title) or "clerical" (entry level jobs).

Education and training: List any job-related training or education, including military. A recent graduate should emphasize special skills and accomplishments that directly relate to doing the job. If your education and training are important parts of your credentials, put them at the top. However, people with five or more years of experience usually place this information at the end of their resumes.

Previous experience: List your most recent job first, then work your way back. Show promotions as separate jobs. Cluster jobs held long ago or not related to your present objective. These could include the part-time jobs you had while going to school.

If you have little work experience, list unpaid work (such as in the family business) and volunteer jobs in place of paid jobs. Always emphasize the skills you used in these experiences that will help you in the job you want now. There is no need to mention that this work was unpaid.

Job gaps: Your list of work experience may have gaps. You may have been going to school, having a child, or working for yourself. Present this time positively. "Self-employed" or "Returned to school to improve my business skills" is better than saying "unemployed."

You can avoid showing you did not have a job at certain times by listing years or seasons. For example, if you didn't work from late January to early March of 1986, you can write:

Job A: 1985-1986   **Job B: 1986-1988**

No one can tell there was a two-month space between jobs.

Job titles: Many people have more responsibilities than their job titles suggest. Some titles are unusual and won't mean much to most people. In these cases, use a title that more accurately tells what you did.

Accomplishments: An employer wants to know what you did well in your work and other experiences. Just as in an interview, list some of your best accomplishments. Emphasize the number of people you served, units produced, staff trained, sales increased, and any other measurable achievements.

Personal data: This is definitely optional. Who cares how tall you are? Or that you like to read romance novels? Some information can be put in this section, but only if it supports the job objective.

References: Don't list references on your resume. If employers want them, they will ask. Even saying "References available on request" at the end of your resume adds nothing. If you have particularly good references, you can say something like, "Excellent references from previous employers are available." This sentence can be in the personal section.

The Skills Resume

The skills resume is sometimes called a *functional* resume. In this resume, your experience is organized under key skills. These are the skills you need to succeed in the job you want. They should also be skills that you are good at and like to use.

Look at the resume on this page. It is an example of a simple skills resume.

ANDREA ATWOOD
3231 East Harbor Road
Grand Rapids, Michigan 41103

Home: (303) 447-2111   Message: (303) 547-8201

Objective: A responsible position in retail sales

Areas of Accomplishment:

Customer Service
- Communicate well with all age groups.
- Able to interpret customer concerns to help them find the items they want.
- Received six Employee of the Month awards in 3 years.

Merchandise Display
- Developed display skills via in-house training and experience.
- Received Outstanding Trainee award for Christmas Toy Display.
- Dress mannequins, arrange table displays, and organize sale merchandise.

Stock Control and Marking
- Maintained and marked stock during department manager's 6-week illness.
- Developed more efficient record-keeping procedures.

Additional Skills
- Operate cash register, IBM compatible hardware, calculators, and electronic typewriters.
- Punctual, honest, reliable, and a hard-working self-starter.

Experience:
Harper's Department Store
Grand Rapids, Michigan
1984 to Present

Education:
Central High School
Grand Rapids, Michigan
3.6/4.0 grade point average
Honor Graduate in Distributive Education

Two years retail sales training in Distributive Education. Also courses in Business Writing, Accounting, Typing, and Word Processing.

By using a skills resume, you can present accomplishments from all your life experiences. It is a good format when you need to "hide" problems that a chronological resume might show. Examples include limited paid work experience, gaps in your job history, and little or no paid work experience in the field you want to get into now.

A well-written skills resume presents your strengths and avoids showing your weaknesses. Some employers don't like them for this reason. They are also harder to write. Still, a skills resume is worthwhile for many people and is worth doing. If you have a good work history, you can combine the best elements of both resume types into a combination resume. Some of the examples at the end of this chapter have done just that. Look them over for ideas to use in your own resume.

Production Tips

Make sure your resume looks good and is error free. It should be typed on a business typewriter or word processor using letter quality type. Dot matrix computer type or sloppy type from an old typewriter is not acceptable.

Most small print shops will have your resume typed, for a fee, if you don't have your own machine. Plan on printing at least a hundred copies. This is not very expensive at most "quick-print" shops. Look in the Yellow Pages for listings.

Pay extra for good quality paper. It is worth every penny. Ivory, white and off-white are conservative colors that look professional.

A Few Words on Resume Experts

If you ask ten people for advice on your resume, they will all be willing to give it. And no two of them will agree. You will have to make up your own mind about your resume. Feel free to break any "rules" if you have a good reason for doing so.

Some of the resumes in the examples break rules. None of them is perfect. However, they are all based on real resumes used by people who wrote them themselves. So look them over, then write your own.

Sample Resumes

Dennis Franz

4431 Old Mill Road
Kansas City, Kansas 66301

(614) 886-4040

(614) 634-5151

CAREER OBJECTIVE: Supervisor of Building Maintenance

SUMMARY: Four years experience in maintaining a $3,000,000 scientific facility that requires exceptionally high standards of security and cleanliness. Two years experience hiring, supervising, and training 24 employees. Reorganized workload to save $22,000/year in salaries and wages.

EMPLOYMENT HISTORY:

The Hadley Research Center, Kansas City, Kansas
Maintenance Supervisor, November 1985 to Present

- Hire, supervise, and train staff.
- Saved $22,000/year by replacing four retiring full-time employees with part-time staff.
- Conduct regular training and refresher courses to keep staff current on equipment and procedures.
- Maintain stringent oversight of safety procedures and hazardous waste disposal.

August 1983 to October 1985
Electronic Specialist

- Maintained complex scientific equipment valued at $1.5 million.
- Cleaned, calibrated, adjusted, rewired, and repaired as needed
- Monitored air and water quality of plant and environs.
- Conducted periodic fire and accident drills. Filed evaluations of each drill with the Hadley Center Director and State Environmental Agency.

EDUCATION:

Associate Degree in Electrical Engineering Technology, Detroit Technical College, Detroit, Michigan Grade Point Average: 3.6 on scale of 4.0

Deborah Levy

4141 Beachway Road
Redondo Beach, California 90277

(213) 449-2279
(213) 540-3152

Objective: Management Position in a Major Hotel

Summary of Experience: Four years experience in sales, catering, banquet services, and guest relations in 300-room hotel. Doubled sales revenues from conferences and meetings. Increased dining room and bar revenues by 44%. Won prestigious national and local awards for increased productivity and services.

Experience:

Park Regency Hotel, Los Angeles, California
Assistant Manager
1986 to Present

- Oversee a staff of 36, including dining room and bar, housekeeping, and public relations operations.
- Introduced new menus and increased dining room revenues by 44%. Gourmet America awarded us their Hotel Haute Cuisine first place award in both 1987 and 1988.
- Attracted 28% more diners with the first revival of Big Band Cocktail Dances in the Los Angeles area.

Kingsmont Hotel, Redondo Beach, California
Sales and Public Relations
1984 to 1986

- Doubled revenues per month from conferences and meetings.
- Redecorated meeting rooms and updated sound and visual media equipment. Trained staff to operate and maintain equipment.
- Instituted Outstanding Employee Courtesy awards, which resulted in an upgrade from B-to AAA-Plus in the Car and Travel Handbook.

Education: Associates Degree in Hotel Management from Henfield College of San Francisco. One year with the Boileau Culinary Institute, where I won the 1984 Grand Prize Scholarship. Bachelor of Arts in English Literature, University of Virginia.

Thomas Welborn

673 Wickham Road
Phoenix, AZ 85009

Home: (602) 253-9678
Leave message: (602) 257-6643

JOB OBJECTIVE

Position in the electronics industry requiring skills in the design, sale, installation, maintenance, and repair of audio, video, and other advanced electronics. Prefer tasks needing creative problem-solving skills and customer contact.

EDUCATION

ITT TECHNICAL INSTITUTE
Phoenix, AZ
A.S. Degree, Electronics Engineering Technology
1987-present

Completed a comprehensive, two-year curriculum including over 2000 hours of class and advanced laboratory. Theoretical, practical, and hands-on knowledge of audio and RF amplifiers, AM/FM transmitter-receiver circuits, OP amplifiers, microwave and radar communications, digital circuits, and much more. Excellent attendance while working part time to pay tuition. Graduating in top 25%.

PLAINS JR. COLLEGE
Phoenix, AZ

Courses included Digital Electronics, Programming, business, and 1986 computer applications. Worked full time and maintained a B+ average.

DESERT VIEW H.S.
1984 graduate

College prep. courses including advanced math, business, marketing, merchandising, computer orientation, and Basic programming. Very active in varsity sports. National Jr. Honor Society for two years.

SKILLS

PROBLEM-SOLVING: Familiar with the underlying theory of most electronic systems and am particularly strong in isolating problems by using logic and persistence. I enjoy the challenge of solving complex problems and will work long hours, if necessary, to do this on a deadline.

INTERPERSONAL: Have supervised five staff and trained many more. Comfortable with one-to-one and small group communications. Can explain technical issues simply to customers of varying levels of sophistication. Had over 10,000 customer contacts in one job with no complaints and several written commendations.

TECHNICAL: Background in a variety of technical areas including medical equipment, consumer electronics, computers, automated cash registers, photocopiers, and standard office and computer equipment and peripherals. Have designed special application combinational and sequential logic circuits using TTL logic. Constructed Z-80 microprocessor and wrote several machine language programs for this system. Can diagnose and repair problems in digital and analog circuits.

ORGANIZATIONAL: Have set up and run my own small business and worked in another responsible job while going to school full time. Earned enough money to live independently and pay all school expenses during this time. I can work independently and have learned to use my time efficiently.

EXPERIENCE

BANDLER'S INN: 1984-present. Waiter, promoted to night manager. Complete responsibility for all operations of a shift grossing over $300,000 in sales per year. Supervised five full-time and three part-time staff. Business increased during my employment by 35% and profits by 42%, much of it due to word of mouth advertising of satisfied customers.

FRANKLIN HOSPITAL: 1983-1984. Electronic Service Technician's Assistant. Worked in Medical, Physics, and Electronics Departments. Assisted technicians in routine service and maintenance of a variety of hospital equipment. Part time while going to school.

TOM'S YARD SERVICE: 1981-1985. Set up a small business while in school. Worked part time and summers doing yard work. Made enough money to buy a car and save for tuition.

LILI LI LU

1536 Sierra Way
Piedmont, California 97435
Telephone 436-3874

OBJECTIVE:

Program development, coordination, and administration.

Especially in a people-oriented organization where there is a need to assure broad cooperation through the use of sound planning and strong administrative and persuasive skills to achieve community goals.

MAJOR AREAS OF EXPERIENCE AND ABILITY

Budgeting and management for sound program development

With partner, established a new association devoted to maximum personal development and self-realization for each of its members. Over a period of time, administered budget totaling $285,000. Jointly planned growth of group and related expenditures, investments, programs, and development of property holdings to realize current and long-term goals. As a result, holdings increased 25 fold over the period, reserves invested increased 1200%, and all major goals for members have been achieved. (A number have been sharply exceeded.)

Purchasing to assure smooth flow of needed supplies and services

Usually alone (but in strong give and take consultation with partner concerning major acquisitions), made most purchasing decisions to assure maximum production from available funds. Maintained continuous stock inventory to determine ongoing needs, selected suppliers, and assured proper disbursements to achieve a strong continuing line of credit while minimizing financing costs. Handled occasional "crash" needs so that no significant project was ever adversely affected by failure to mobilize necessary supplies, equipment, or services on time.

Personal development and motivation

From the beginning, developed resources to assure maximum progress in achieving potential for development among all members of our group. Frequently engaged in intensive personnel counseling to achieve this. Sparked new community programs to help accomplish such results. Although arrangements with my partner gave me no say in selecting new members (I took them as they came), the results produced by this effort are a source of strong and continuing satisfaction to me (see "specific results" below).

Transportation management

Jointly with partner determined transportation needs of our group and, in consultation with members, assured specific transportation equipment acquisitions over a broad range of types (including seagoing). Contracted for additional transportation when necessary. Assured maximum utilization of limited motor pool to meet often-conflicting requirements demanding arrival of the same vehicle at widely divergent points at the same moment. Negotiated resolution of such conflicts in the best interest of all concerned. In addition, arranged four major moves of all facilities, furnishings, and equipment to new locations — two across the country.

Other functions performed

Duties periodically require my action in the following additional functions: crisis management, proposal preparation, political analysis, nutrition, recreation planning and administration, stock market operations, taxes, building and ground maintenance, community organization, social affairs administration (including VIP entertaining), catering, landscaping (two awards for excellence), contract negotiations, teaching and more.

Some specific results

Above experience gained in 20 years devoted to family development and household management in partnership with my husband, Harvey Hwangchung Lu, who is equally responsible for results produced. Primary achievements: Son Lee, 19, honor student at Harvard majoring in physics, state forensics champion. Daughter Su, 18, leading candidate for the U.S. Olympic team in gymnastics, entering prelaw studies at the University of California, Berkeley, this fall, Son Kwan, 16, a senior at Piedmont High School with 3.98 average, president of the student council, organizer and leader of a highly successful rock band, but heavily disposed toward future studies in oceanography. Secondary achievements: A lovely home in Piedmont (social center for area teenagers). Vacation homes in Newport, Oregon (on the beach) and a cabin in Big Sur. President of Piedmont High School PTA two years. Organized a successful citizen protest to stop incursion of Oakland commercialism on Piedmont area. Appointed by Robert F. Kennedy as coordinator of his campaign in Oakland.

Personal data and other facts

Born in 1934. Often complimented on appearance. Bachelor of Arts (Asian History), Cody College, Cody, California. Highly active in community affairs. Have learned that there is a spark of genius in almost everyone, which, when nurtured, can flare into dramatic achievement.

Adapted from <u>Who's Hiring Who?</u>, by Richard Lathrop, Ten Speed Press, 1987.

Cover Letters

This type of letter was originally called a cover letter because it went along with, and covered, a resume. Different situations need different types of letters. The sample cover letters in this chapter give examples based on typical situations. Look them over for ideas when writing your own letters.

You may find that you don't need to send many formal letters. Many job seekers get by with informal thank you notes sent with copies of resumes and JIST Cards. But certain types of jobs and some organizations require a more formal approach. Use your judgment.

As always, make certain that all your job-search correspondence makes a good impression. Following are some additional tips on cover letters.

Send it to someone by name: Get the name of the person who is most likely to supervise you. Call first to get an interview. Then send your letter and resume.

Get it right: Make sure you spell their name correctly and use their correct title. Any error in spelling or grammar will create a poor impression.

Be clear about what you want: If you want an interview, ask for it. If you are interested in that organization, say so. Give clear reasons why they should consider you.

Be friendly: A professional, informal style is usually best. Avoid a hard-sell "Hire me now!" approach. No ones likes to be pushed.

Make it look good: Just as with a resume, any correspondence to an employer must look good. Use good quality paper and matching envelopes. A standard business format is good for most letters. Use a good quality typewriter!

Target your letter: Typical reasons for sending a cover letter include: responding to an ad, preparing an employer for an interview (the best reason!), and following up after a phone call or interview. Each of these letters will be different.

Follow up: Remember that contacting an employer directly is much more effective than a letter. Don't expect a letter to get you many interviews. They are best used to follow up *after* you have contacted the employer.

Sample Cover Letters

8990 Harcourt Way
Anderson, Arkansas 71012
August 17, 1993

Charles R. Hanna
Operations Manager
Doyle Trucking Company
Kansas City, Kansas 60641

Dear Mr. Hanna:

I obtained your name from the membership directory of the Affiliated Trucking Outlook Association. I have been a member for over ten years and I am very active in the Southeast Region. The reason I am writing is to ask your help. The firm I had been employed with has been bought by a larger corporation. The operations here have been disbanded, leaving me unemployed.

Although I like where I live, I know that finding a position at the level of responsibility I seek may require a move. As a center of the transportation business, your city is one of those I have targeted for special attention. A copy of my resume is enclosed for your use.

I'd like you to review it and consider where a person with my background might get a good reception in Kansas City. Perhaps you could think of a specific person for me to contact?

I have specialized in fast-growing organizations or ones that have experienced rapid change. My particular strength is bringing things under control, then increasing profits. While my resume does not state this, I have excellent references from my former employer and would have stayed if a similar position existed at their new location.

As a member of the association, I hoped that you would provide some special attention to my request for assistance. Please call my answering service collect if you have any immediate leads. I am coming to Kansas City on a job-hunting trip within the next six weeks. Prior to then I will call you for advice on who I might contact for interviews. Even if they have no jobs open for me now, perhaps they will know of someone else who might!

Thanks in advance for your help on this.

Sincerely,

Alan J. Harmon

Alan J. Harmon
Treasurer, Southeast Region
Affiliated Trucking Association

Apartment A35
4085 Larchmont Road
Seattle, WA 97033
September 1, 1988

The Seattle News Sentinel
Box N9142
1414 East New York Street
Seattle, WA 97002

Your advertisement for an Administrative Secretary could have been written with me in mind. I have had three years experience in a busy office where time management, communications skills, and ability to deal with all kinds of people are vital.

Directing junior secretarial staff, writing customer service letters, and preparing monthly, quarterly, and yearly sales reports are my responsibilities. I regularly use computer software packages to track and maintain our sales revenues and customer mailing lists.

For your consideration, I have enclosed a resume that more completely describes my education and experience. I look forward to meeting with you soon.

Sincerely,

Susan Deming

Susan Deming

3321 East Haverford Road
Fort Wayne, Indiana 48011
October 15, 1990

Mr. Howard R. Lindsey
Chief Engineer
WXLC TV
10212 North Oxford Avenue
Fort Wayne, Indiana 48020

Dear Mr. Lindsey:

Thank you for agreeing to meet with me at 3 p.m. on November 5 to talk about job opportunities for Broadcast Technicians. Although I understand that you have no openings right now, I'm enclosing my resume to give you some information about my training and background.

You will see that I have worked on both up-to-the-minute and almost "antique" equipment. Working part time for a small station in Gary, I've learned to monitor, adjust, and repair a variety of equipment—some dating from the 1950s. I believe learning to coax the old equipment into operating has been invaluable experience. At Gary Junior College, I have become the person to call if their new state-of-the-art audio and video equipment doesn't seem to be performing as it should.

I look forward to graduating and devoting full time to my career. Your help is greatly appreciated, particularly your invitation to spend some time observing field operations during your live election coverage.

Sincerely,

Linda A. Jontz

Linda A. Jontz

1768 S. Carrollton St.
Nashville, TN 96050
May 26, 1992

Ms. Karen Miller
Office Manager
Lendon, Lendon and Sears
Suite 101, Landmark Building
Summit, NJ 11736

Dear Ms. Miller:

Enclosed is a copy of my resume which describes my work experience as a legal assistant. I hope this information will be helpful as background for our interview next Monday at 4 o'clock.

I appreciated your taking time to describe your requirements so fully. This sounds like a position that could develop into a satisfying career. And my training in accounting—along with experience using a variety of computer programs—seems to match your needs.

Lendon, Lendon and Sears is a highly respected name in New Jersey. I am excited about this opportunity and I look forward to meeting with you.

Sincerely,

Richard Wittenberg

Richard Wittenberg

GETTING A
JOB IS A JOB

Organizing Your Time

You now know more about finding a job than most people in North America. But the methods work only if you use them!

To find a job fast, you must:

- Have a clear job objective
- Know how to get interviews
- Know what to do once you get there
- Get as many interviews as you can

The more interviews you get, the sooner you will get a job offer. If you spend six hours a day looking for a job, you are very likely to find a job sooner than if you spent only two hours.

The average job seeker gets about two interviews per week. At that rate, it takes an average of three to four months to find a job. The following chart shows how many interviews the average job seeker needs to get a job.

The Average Job Seeker Gets:				
Interviews per Week	X	# Weeks Unemployed	=	Total # of Interviews
2	X	12	=	24

If you get twice the average number of interviews per week (only four interviews!), you could cut your job-search time in half. Many people who use the methods taught in this book have done just that.

This chapter helps you organize your job search. To begin, here is the secret of success. Devote as much time and energy to *getting* a job as you will once you have it. In a sense, getting a job is a job.

Setting Up Your Job-Search Office

To organize your job search as if it were a job, you need a place where you can work. Usually, this will be a place in your home set aside as your job search office. The following are some ideas to help you set up this office.

A telephone: It is very important that you have a telephone. If you don't have one, set up your office in the home of a friend or relative who has a phone.

Basic furniture: You will need a table or desk to write on, a chair, and enough space to store your materials.

A quiet place: Just as on a job, you must have a place where you can concentrate. If you have children, arrange for someone else to care for them during your "office hours." Ask family or friends to contact you at other times. It is best to select a place where you can safely leave your materials. Then you won't have to set up your work space every day.

Materials you will need:

- A good ink pen, black ink if possible
- Several pencils with erasers
- Lined paper for notes, contact lists, and other uses
- 3" x 5" cards for use as job lead cards
- Small 3" x 5" card file box with dividers
- Thank you notes and envelopes
- Resumes and JIST Cards
- Business-size envelopes
- Stamps
- Yellow Pages phone book
- Calendars and planning schedules
- A copy of this book, of course

Is there anything else you need? If so, continue your list here:_____

_____

_____

_____

Special Forms and Systems

This section provides you with special forms and ways to organize your job search.

Job-Lead Cards

By using the job-search methods you have learned in this book, you can develop hundreds of contacts. Keeping track of all this is more than your memory can handle. Look at the following 3" x 5" card. It shows the kinds of information you can keep about each person who helps you in your job search.

> **Organization:** _Mutual Health Insurance_
> **Contact Person:** _Anna Tomey_ **Phone:** _317-355-0216_
> **Source of Lead:** _Aunt Ruth_
> **Notes:** _4/10 Called. Anna on vacation. Callback 4/15 4/15 Interview set 4/20 at 1:30. 4/20 Anna showed me around. They use the same computers we used in school! (Friendly people) Sent Thank You note + Tist Card call back 5/1. 5/1 Second interview 5/8 at 9 a.m.!_

Although the card used in this example is specially printed, you can keep the same kind of information on blank 3" x 5" cards available at most department and stationery stores. Plan on using at least a hundred of these cards.

Create one card for each person who gave you a referral or is a possible employer. Keep brief notes each time you talk with them to help you remember important details for your next contact.

Follow-Up Box

Most department and stationery stores have small boxes made to hold 3" x 5" cards. They also have tabbed dividers for these boxes. Buy an inexpensive card file box and enough dividers to set up a box as described here.

Set up a divider for each day of the month, numbering them 1 through 31. Once this has been done, file each completed Job Lead Card under the date you want to follow up on it.

Example 1: You get the name of a referral to call, but you can't get to them right away. You create a Job Lead Card and file it under tomorrow's date.

Example 2: You call someone from a Yellow Pages listing, but they are busy this week. They tell you to call back in two weeks. You file their Job Lead Card under the date exactly two weeks in the future.

Example 3: You get an interview with a person who doesn't have any jobs now, but he gives you a name of someone else who might. After you send a thank you note, you file his Job Lead Card under a date a few weeks in the future.

As you contact more and more people in your job search, the number of people you file away for future follow up will keep increasing. You will find more and more "new" leads as you follow up with people you've already contacted one or more times in the past. This is one of the most effective ways of getting a job!

At the beginning of each week, you simply review all the Job Lead Cards you filed for this week. On your weekly schedule, list any interviews or follow-up calls you promised for a particular time and date.

At the beginning of each day, pull the Job Lead Cards filed under that date. List them on your daily contact list sheet (described in the following section) for that day.

The Daily Contact Sheet

This is a simple form you can make on regular lined sheets of paper. Complete one of these forms each day. I suggest that you list at least 20 people or organizations to contact before you begin any phone calls that day. Use any source to get these leads—referrals, Yellow Pages, want ads, and so on. The sample that follows will give you an idea of how the form works.

Daily Contact Sheet

Contact Name / Organization	Referral Source	Job Lead Card	Phone Number
1. *The Flower Shoppe*	*Yellow Pages*	*Yes*	*897-6041*
2. *Rainbow Flowers*	*" "*	*Yes*	*253-7365*
3. *Hartley Nurseries*	*John Lee*	*Yes*	*661-2224*
4. *Posies, Etc.*	*In the Neighborhood*		*778-6640*
5. *Plants To Go*	*Want Ad*	*Yes*	*835-7016*

Your Weekly Job-Search Schedule

The steps that follow will help you organize each week of your job search to get the most from your time.

Step 1: How Many Hours Per Week?

How many hours per week do you plan to spend looking for a job?

In most cases, I recommend about 25 hours per week for a person who is looking for full-time work. An active job search is difficult work, and 40 hours per week is too much for many people. Since the average job seeker spends about five hours per week actively looking for work, this is much more than the average. Whatever you decide is fine. You should realize that the less time you spend, the longer you are likely to be unemployed.

On the following line, write the number of hours per week you plan to spend looking for work.

Number of Hours Per Week to Spend Looking for a Job: _____

Step 2: On What Days?

Decide what days each week you will use to look for work. Since most businesses are open Monday through Friday, these are often the best days to look. In the first column of the following form, check the days you plan to use for your job search. Don't mark in the other columns yet.

Check Days	Number of Hours	Times
_____ Monday	_____	_____ to _____
		_____ to _____
_____ Tuesday	_____	_____ to _____
		_____ to _____
_____ Wednesday	_____	_____ to _____
		_____ to _____
_____ Thursday	_____	_____ to _____
		_____ to _____
_____ Friday	_____	_____ to _____
		_____ to _____
_____ Saturday	_____	_____ to _____
		_____ to _____
_____ Sunday	_____	_____ to _____
		_____ to _____

Total number of hours per week _____

Step 3: How Many Hours Per Day?

Using the form you've already started, decide how many hours you will spend looking for work on each of the days you selected. For example, if you selected Mondays, you may decide to spend five hours on Mondays looking for work. You would then write "5" in the "Number of Hours" column of the form. Do this with all the days you checked until the total equals the number of hours per week you listed in Step 1.

Step 4: What Times Each Day?

Using the same form, use the remaining column "Times" to list the times you will use each day to look for work. For example, if you decided to spend six hours each Monday looking for work, you might decide to begin at 8 a.m. and work till noon (4 hours), take an hour off for lunch, then work from 1 p.m. to 3 p.m. (2 hours).

Step 5: Create a Weekly Job-Search Schedule

Use the form shown here to mark off the days and times you've scheduled each week to look for a job. The sample shows how you can make your own schedule.

	Sunday	Monday	Tuesday	Wednesday	Thursday	Friday	Saturday
8:00		Get organized for the day				→	
8:30	Read want	Gather old & New job	}				↑
9:00	ads	leads	} ————			→	
9:30	↓		}				
10:00		Make phone Contacts	————			→	
10:30		follow up & get 2	}				
11:00		interviews	} ————			→	
11:30		Write/Send		}		→	
12:00		follow up correspondence		} ————			day
12:30		Plan afternoon ————————				→	Off!
1:00		Lunch ————————				→	
1:30					Appt. with Lisa at Welch		
2:00			Leave for IV		Whitman & Scott		
2:30			↓				
3:00			Interview		Drop by State Employment	Go to printers for resume	
3:30			at Fischer Brothers		Office		
4:00		Work on resume ———→		Make final revisions			
4:30		↓		of resume Proof Read!	Take resume to printers	Afternoon	
5:00	Dinner ———————————————→					Off!	
5:30							↓
6:00	Read job	}					
6:30	Search books	} ———————————→					

126   Getting a Job Is a Job

	Sunday	Monday	Tuesday	Wednesday	Thursday	Friday	Saturday
8:00							
8:30							
9:00							
9:30							
10:00							
10:30							
11:00							
11:30							
12:00							
12:30							
1:00							
1:30							
2:00							
2:30							
3:00							
3:30							
4:00							
4:30							
5:00							
5:30							
6:00							
6:30							

Your Daily Job-Search Schedule

You have decided what days and what hours to spend on your job search. But what will you do each day? You still need a daily plan to get the most out of each hour. Look at the following sample daily plan. Yours may look different, but you should use many of the same ideas on your own daily schedule.

Sample Daily Schedule

7:00 — 8:00		Get up, shower, dress, and eat breakfast
8:00 — 8:15		Organize my work space; review schedule for interviews or promised follow-ups; update schedule as needed
8:15 — 9:00		Review old leads for follow-up (from follow up box); develop new leads (want ads, Yellow Pages, warm contact lists, and so on); complete daily contact list
9:00 — 10:00		Make phone calls
10:00 — 10:15		Take a break!
10:15 — 11:00		Make phone calls
11:00 — 12:00		Send follow-up notes as needed
12:00 — 1:00		Lunch break
1:00 — 3:00		Go on interviews, cold contacts in the field, research for interviews at library

Some Tips for Your Schedule

Set daily objectives for interviews: Remember that we have redefined an interview. An interview now includes seeing people who hire people like you but don't necessarily have a job opening. Don't stop calling until you have met your daily objective!

Your goal should be to get at least one interview per day. Many people get two interviews per day if they use the techniques I suggest. Over a four-week period of five-day weeks, that adds up to 40 interviews! That is more interviews than the average job seeker gets in four months. It is no wonder they are unemployed so long!

Expect to get rejected: You will need to make 10 to 15 phone calls to get one interview. Most people can make that many calls in an hour, so two hours of calls can result in two interviews. The calls that don't get you an interview are often friendly. So the rejection you experience is really no big deal.

Make phone calls, be active: You won't get a job by reading job-search books or working on your resume. Save those activities for other times. During the day, concentrate on active job search methods.

Stick to your schedule: Arrange interviews at times other than those you planned to spend in your job-search office. Plan to take care of your personal business after your office hours, too.

Don't get discouraged: Looking for a job is hard work, so take time for breaks. And take time to take care of yourself.

If you follow these recommendations, you will soon have the job you want. In Chapter Fourteen you'll see how to make a good beginning at your new job—and how to make the most of each opportunity to grow and succeed.

ON THE ROAD
TO SUCCESS

New-Job Survival Skills and Getting Ahead

During the years you work you are likely to have many different jobs. Each one will present chances to learn and problems to overcome.

As you begin a new job, you will probably feel a bit of fear. Often, you don't know what to expect:

- Will you get along with the other people who work there?
- Are you dressed right?
- Will you be able to handle the new responsibilities?

These and other concerns will be on your mind as you begin a new job. This chapter has been written to help you get off to a successful start. You also will find important information on how to get ahead once you are on the job.

Surviving on the Job

There are things you can do to increase your chances of success on a new job. If you want to do well, you may need to change the way you act and some of your attitudes.

Why People Get Fired

Look at the following list of reasons people have been fired. Check the top three reasons you think *employers* gave for firing an employee.

_____ Unable to get along with other workers
_____ Dishonest
_____ Poor dress or grooming
_____ Unreliable, too many days absent or late
_____ Used work time for personal business
_____ Couldn't do the work
_____ Worked too slowly, made too many mistakes
_____ Would not follow orders, did not get along with supervisor
_____ Abused alcohol or drugs
_____ Misrepresented their skills or experience
_____ Too many accidents, did not follow safety rules

A Review of the Reasons People are Fired

Unable to get along with other workers: Employers do not give this as one of the top three reasons for firing someone. But workers consider this problem one of the top reasons they don't like their jobs. You don't have to like all the people you work with, but it is important that you get along with them.

Dishonesty: This is one of the top reasons employers give for firing someone. More employers are now screening new applicants to eliminate people who have been dishonest with previous employers. If you picked this as one of the top three reasons, you are correct! Employers don't want to pay someone who steals from them or can't be trusted.

Poor dress or grooming: The way you look is very important. This is particularly true in office jobs and in jobs where you deal with customers. Many employers will not tell you directly that your dress or grooming is a problem. But this problem will affect how the employer feels about you. You may not be given very much responsibility, for example. Employers don't give dress and grooming as top reasons for firing someone. But this can be one of many problems a terminated employee had.

Unreliable, too many days absent or late: When an employee is absent, it disrupts the work of other people. They may have to neglect their work to make up for the absent worker. Now two or more people are behind in their work. People who are often late set a bad example for others. And, depending on the job, they can disrupt the work of other people. Employers place these problems high on their list of reasons for firing people.

Couldn't do the work: Few people get fired because they could not do the work. Employers tend to hire people they think can do the job, and then give them time to learn it.

Worked too slowly, made too many mistakes: This is a major reason for job failure. It is one of the top three reasons employers give for firing people. You can see why: unproductive employees cost more than they earn! A slow worker is expensive compared to another worker who gets the same job done in less time.

Workers who make mistakes can be costly in many ways. Perhaps another employee has to spend time correcting errors. A customer may become dissatisfied with the company's products or services as a result of sloppy work. That customer doesn't come back—and tells others not to!

Would not follow orders, did not get along with supervisor: In a battle with a supervisor, you will almost always lose! In fact, this is one of the top three reasons people get fired.

Abuse of alcohol or drugs: Substance abuse has become a major problem at some companies. But it is not among the top three reasons for being fired. This may be because a person who abuses alcohol or drugs gets fired for being unreliable or some other reason. The employer may not even know the cause of the problem.

Too many accidents, did not follow safety rules: Employers do not want to keep people who have "accidents" or who do not follow safety rules. Accidents can be costly to employers and to other employees. Fortunately, most people follow good safety rules. This is not among the top reasons employers give for firing people.

More Reasons

There are many reasons a company might fire a person. Almost any reason can be enough if it is a serious problem for that company. More often, however, people are fired for more than one reason. For example, they may be late to work too often and make too many mistakes in their work.

In the following spaces, list at least three other reasons an employer might have to fire someone. Perhaps you know someone who was fired. Or can think of a reason you might fire someone.

1. _____

_____

2. _____

_____

3. _____

_____

Getting Off to a Good Start: Some Things You Can Do— and Some Things You Should Not Do

Now you know why most people get fired. But that doesn't tell you what you can do to be successful. This section offers tips you can use to get started and succeed in a new job. Many of these tips have been used by people who have done well in their jobs.

As you read these suggestions, use the space below each tip to write notes about how you could use each one. Sample notes are provided for the first few tips to give you ideas for your own. Use extra paper if you need more space for your notes.

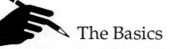 The Basics

There is no such thing as a "dead end job": Learn all you can from any job you have! Do it as well as you are able. Look for chances to expand the job to put your skills to better use. Even if you are not able to move up in this organization, a "dead end" job can give you a good reference for a different position.

1. *If I take a survival job until I finish school, try to get into the same type of industry in an entry level job.*

2. *Let the boss and the personnel department know I'm going to school and want to move to a different job within the company when I'm done.*

Write your own notes here: _____

_____

_____

_____

_____

Don't miss work: A minor illness (like a cold) is not a good reason for missing work. Nor are most personal problems (such as child care). If you miss more than three days a year for these reasons, it may be too much. Even if you get "sick" time. You can call attention to yourself in a negative way if you miss too many days—for any reason. A new employee cannot afford this kind of attention.

1. *Call Aunt Alice to see if she would watch the kids if one gets sick and can't go to school.*

2. *Try to have no absences at all during my first year on the job.*

_____

Write your own notes here: _____

_____

_____

_____

_____

Be on time: There are very few acceptable reasons for being late. Usually, being late is your own fault and could have been avoided. For example, "I missed the bus" and "I ran out of gas" are poor excuses. You could easily have avoided either mishap. Identify the reasons you are most likely to be late and eliminate them.

Write your own notes here: _____

_____

_____

_____

_____

Call if you will be absent or late: If you will be more than a few minutes late or absent for any reason, call in at the beginning of the work day. Talk directly to your supervisor and explain the situation. Do not leave a message. Sometimes, you may be able to call the day before if you think there could be a problem.

Write your own notes here: _____

_____

_____

_____

_____

Be neat and clean: Be careful about your grooming. Be aware of how you look at all times. It is important that your clothes fit well and are clean and pressed. Notice how others dress in jobs similar to yours. Dress at least as well, but cleaner. Write some ideas about the outfits you have that you can use on the job. Wear some of these and ask others how they think you look.

Write your own notes here: _____

_____

_____

_____

_____

Find a "buddy" to help you: New employees are often assigned a co-worker to teach the basics of the job. If you are not assigned a buddy, ask for one. After you are there a few days, look for someone you think you will get along with. If they know the work, ask them to help you out. Go out of your way to be nice to this person!

Write your own notes here: _____

_____

_____

Read personnel and procedure manuals: Large organizations have books that give the rules for working there and instructions for doing various parts of the job. Ask your supervisor for these and read them as soon as possible. Most small organizations will not have these manuals. You will need to ask your supervisor to explain any special procedures or rules to you.

Write your own notes here: _____

_____

_____

_____

_____

Stay away from *problem* employees: Some people in any organization tend to be negative about their jobs. Others do things against the rules, waste time, or in other ways are not good workers. They may even be fun to be with. But spending time with them will affect your job. Your co-workers and supervisors may begin to see YOU as a "problem." Be friendly. But do not socialize with people like this any more than necessary.

Write your own notes here: _____

_____

_____

_____

_____

Keep personal problems at home: You are paid to get a job done. Do not spend time on personal concerns if you can avoid it. Making personal phone calls, paying bills, coming back late from lunch, talking to other staff about what you did last weekend, or getting to work late because the car ran out of gas (or whatever) are not what you are being paid to do.

Although some socializing on the job is common, you can easily overdo it. Limit your personal activities and discussions to breaks, lunch times, or hours outside of work as much as possible.

Write your own notes here: _____

_____

_____

_____

_____

Children: They may be the most important part of your life, but their care is not the concern of an employer. If you expect to work full time, you must find ways to separate family responsibilities from your role as an employee. Arrange child care so that you do not miss work when they are ill. Strongly discourage phone calls except in emergencies. When interviewing for a job, tell employers that you will be a dependable worker and that child care has been arranged. Assure them that you needn't miss work for this reason.

Write your own notes here: _____

_____

_____

_____

_____

Work fast, but carefully: It is important to work at a steady and quick pace. Find a pace that you can keep up all day without making errors. Correcting mistakes just wastes time later. But this way of working requires concentration. You will need to make good use of breaks and lunch periods for rest.

Write your own notes here: _____

_____

_____

_____

_____

Advanced Tips

Following these basic tips will help you get off to a good start. If you want to be promoted or have more control over what you do on your job, there are additional things you can do. Again, use the space following each tip to write notes on how you can best use it.

Dress and groom for a promotion: If you want to get ahead in an organization, dress and groom as if you work at the level you hope to reach next. This is not always possible, but at the very least, be clean and well-groomed. Wear clothes that fit well and look good on you. Copy the clothing styles of others in the organization who are successful. Even when your co-workers see you away from work, present the image you want for yourself at work.

Write your own notes here: _____

_____

_____

_____

_____

Be early and stay late: Get to work 15 minutes early each day. Use this time to list what you plan to get done that day. At the end of the day, leave a few minutes after quitting time. Be willing to stay late to meet an important deadline. If you do stay late, let the boss know! Although you should try *never* to be late to work, stay late only when you have an important deadline to meet.

Write your own notes here: _____

_____

_____

_____

_____

Be enthusiastic: Go out of your way to find ways to enjoy your job. Tell others what you like about it, particularly those you work with. Emphasize those parts of your job that you like to do and do well. Share this enthusiasm even in conversations with your friends. Make a particular effort to tell your supervisor what you like about your job. This will help you focus on the parts of your job you are most likely to want to do more of. It will also help others notice that you do them well.

1. *Keep a list of the things on my job that I like to do. Concentrate on doing these things better.*

2. *Ask for additional training on these, get books on them if available, spend time after hours learning about them.*

3. *Ask the boss to assign me more of the type of work I like to do.*

Write your own notes here: _____

_____

_____

_____

_____

Ask for more responsibility: As soon as you begin a new job, look for ways to learn new things. Volunteer to help out in ways you feel will make you more valuable to the organization. Let the boss know you want to move up. And ask for advice about what you can do to be more valuable to the organization.

Write your own notes here: _____

_____

_____

_____

_____

Ask how you can earn more money: In your first week on the job, ask your supervisor to see you for about 30 minutes of private time. When you have their attention, say that you want to be more valuable to the organization. Ask what you can do to get a raise as soon as possible. Request special assignments to help develop your skills.

Before you leave, ask for a specific future date to go over your progress and what you have to do to get the raise. Ask the boss to give you feedback on your progress from time to time.

Write your own notes here: _____

_____

_____

_____

_____

Ask for training: Get as much training as possible! Even if it is outside your job responsibilities, request training the organization provides if it sounds at all useful or interesting. Also define the type of training you need to do your job better, and look for it outside the organization. Explain to your supervisor how the training will help the organization. Ask for help in finding the best training source.

Write your own notes here: _____

_____

_____

_____

_____

Take on difficult projects: You won't get much attention unless you do more than is expected of you. Look for projects you think you can do well and that would benefit the organization in some clear way. Don't promise too much and keep a low profile while you do the work. If no one expects too much, it is easier to be seen as successful, even if your results are not as good as you had hoped.

Write your own notes here: _____

_____

_____

Get measurable results: Keep records of what you do. Compare them to past performance or the average performance of others in similar situations. If your results look good, send a report to your supervisor. For example, if the number of orders went up 40% over the same month last year with no increase in staff, that's a big accomplishment. Look for ways to present what you do in numbers, such as:

Dollars saved
Percent of increased sales
Number of persons served
Number of units processed
Size of budget

Don't just quit: If the job does not seem to be working out for you, ask for a job change within the organization before you give up. If you do decide to leave, give 30 days notice if at all possible. Remember that your next employer will want to contact your previous ones, so do be as friendly as possible in your final days.

Write your own notes here: _____

_____

_____

_____

_____

And Now, In Conclusion. . .

This book now comes to an end. But, for you, there is so much more to come. The final lessons I can offer are these:

Trust yourself. No one can know you better than you.

Decide to do something worthwhile. Whether it is raising a family or saving the whales, believe in something you do as special, as lasting, as valuable.

Work well. All work is worth doing, so put your energy into it and do it as well as you are able.

Enjoy life. It's sort of the same as having fun but lasts longer and means more.

Send thank you notes. Many people will help you throughout your life, in large and small ways. Let them know you appreciate them. The more you give, the more you seem to get in return.

Thank you for reading this book. I wish you good fortune in your job search and your life.

Other Titles Available From

JIST publishes a variety of books on careers and job search topics. Please consider ordering one or more from your dealer, local bookstore, or directly from JIST.

Orders from individuals: Please use the form below (or provide the same information) to order additional copies of this or other books listed on this page. You are also welcome to send us your order (please enclose money order or check) or, if paying with a credit card, simply call our toll free number at **1-800-648-JIST** or **1-317-264-3720**. Our FAX number is **1-317-264-3709**. **Qualified schools and organizations** may request our catalog and obtain information on quantity discounts (we have over 400 career-related books, videos, software, and other items). Our offices are open weekdays 8 a.m. to 5 p.m. local time and our address is:

JIST Works, Inc. • 720 North Park Avenue • Indianapolis, IN 46202-3431

QUANTITY	BOOK TITLE	TOTAL($)
————	**Getting the Job You Really Want**, J. Michael Farr • ISBN: 0-942784-15-4 • **$9.95**	————
————	**The Very Quick Job Search**: Get a Good Job in Less Time, J. Michael Farr • ISBN 0-942784-72-3 • **$9.95**	————
————	**America's 50 Fastest Growing Jobs**: An Authoritative Information Source • ISBN 0-942784-61-8 • **$9.95**	————
————	**America's Top 300 Jobs**: A Complete Career Handbook (trade version of the Occupational Outlook Handbook) • ISBN 0-942784-826-X • **$17.95**	————
————	**America's Federal Jobs**: A Complete Directory of Federal Career Opportunities • ISBN 0-942784-81-2 • **$14.95**	————
————	**The Resume Solution**: How to Write and Use a Resume That Gets Results, David Swanson • ISBN 942784-44-8 • **$10.95**	————
————	**The Job Doctor**: Good Advice on Getting a Good Job, Dr. Phillip Norris, Ph.D. • ISBN 0-942784-43-X • **$8.95**	————
————	**The Right Job for You**: An Interactive Career Planning Guide, J. Michael Farr • ISBN 0-942784-73-1 • **$9.95**	————
————	**Exploring Careers**: A Young Person's Guide to over 300 Jobs • ISBN 0-942784-27-8 • **$19.95**	————
————	**Work in the New Economy**: Careers and Job Seeking into the 21st Century, Robert Wegmann • ISBN 0-942784-19-7 • **$14.95**	————
————	**The Occupational Outlook Handbook** • ISBN 0-942784-38-3 • **$17.95**	————
————	**The Career Connection**: Guide to College Majors and Their Related Careers, Dr. Fred Rowe • ISBN 0-942784-82-0 • **$15.95**	————
————	**The Career Connection II**: Guide to Technical Majors and Their Related Careers, Dr. Fred Rowe • ISBN 0-942784-83-9 • **$13.95**	————

Subtotal ————

Sales Tax ————

Shipping: ($3 for first book, $1 for each additional book.) ————

(U.S. Currency only) **TOTAL ENCLOSED WITH ORDER** ————
(Prices subject to change without notice)

❏ Check ❏ Money order ❏ Credit Card: ❏ MasterCard ❏ VISA ❏ AMEX

Card # (If Applies)_____Exp. Date_____

Name (Please Print)_____

Name of Organization (if applies)_____

Address_____

City/State/Zip_____

Daytime Telephone (   )_____-_____

Thank you for your order!